Gothick
DEVON

Belinda Whitworth

Shire Publications Ltd

Contents

Introduction 3
Using this book 6
A gazetteer of Gothick places 7
Further reading 55
Index 56

For Frog

Printed in Great Britain by CIT Printing Services, Press Buildings, Merlins Bridge, Haverfordwest, Dyfed SA61 1XF.

British Library Cataloguing in Publication Data:
Whitworth, Belinda. Gothick Devon.
–(Gothick Guides; No. 5). I. Title II. Series 914.23504
ISBN 0-7478-0199-1

Series Editor: Jennifer Westwood

Acknowledgements

Thanks are due to the following for answering my queries with such patience: Sue Conniff and other staff of the Devon and Exeter Institution; Exeter Central Library; the West Country Studies Library; Barnstaple Tourist Information Office; Dartmoor National Park; Totnes Tourist Information Office; the Reverend and Mrs R. Varty, Appledore; the Pilchard Inn, Burgh Island; the Northmore Arms, Wonson; the Rock Garden and Nursery, Chudleigh; the Pack o' Cards, Combe Martin; the Warden, Lydford Gorge; the Stag Inn, Rackenford; the Vicar, Weare Giffard. Special thanks to Brian le Messurier and Jennifer Westwood for being so generous with their knowledge and to Katie and Jonathan Fischel for their encouragement.

The photographs are acknowledged as follows: Cadbury Lamb, pages 9, 10, 12, 15, 16, 17, 18, 19, 21, 23, 27 (left), 33, 34, 37, 39, 41, 43, 44 (top), 45, 47, 49, 50, 51, 52 and 53. The remaining photographs are by the author. The line drawings are by Rachel Beckett and the map on pages 4 and 5 is by Robert Dizon.

Introduction

In 1756 the *Gentleman's Magazine* complained that a 'party of gentleman and ladies would sooner travel to the south of France and back again than down to Falmouth (in Cornwall)'. This was partly because of the roads, described thirty years earlier as '...all mud,which rises, spues, and squeezes into the Ditches'. Thus in spite of the fact that Exeter was at one time the fourth or fifth most important city in the realm, Devon as a whole developed apart.

Belief in the supernatural continued long after it was scoffed at elsewhere. As the old rhyme says:

> There's piskies up to Dartymoor
> And t'idden gude yu sez there b'aint.

As late as 1953 the *Western Morning News* wrote of three magistrates who had died from a curse laid upon them by a woman they had sentenced. And the Devil was always a very real and very frightening figure, hiding his cloven feet under long coats, disguising himself as a traveller's friend, kidnapping unbaptised babies or leading a wild hunt.

In parsons, the isolation seems to have bred most un-parsonlike activities. One vicar from Prawle is said to have stopped in mid-sermon to lead his congregation in looting a wrecked ship, with the words, 'Let's all start fair.' Eighteenth-century Joseph Dommett from Bovey Tracey, famed as a wrestler, engaged the leader of a food riot in single-handed combat, later pleading successfully for his acquittal, saying, 'So muscular a man should not be hanged as a felon — it would be sheer waste, for I could not myself have held him, had he had his belly full.' Robert Stephen Hawker from Plymouth is said to have worn wading-boots, crimson gloves, a pink hat and a poncho. More than one dabbled in black magic.

If the men of Devon were once called giants, the county's women are not inconsiderable and some of them hold sway even after their deaths. Madam Gould, who became a great landowner by her own efforts, died and shortly afterwards confronted an apple-stealer in her orchard and later chased a hapless carpenter when he opened her tomb. Lady Mary Howard is condemned to take the shape of a dog and pick a blade of grass every night; her only crime was that she was beautiful, rich and clever. The opening of Joanna Southcott's box of prophecies 'for the millennium' is still eagerly awaited.

Much of Devon's countryside has changed little for hundreds, even thousands, of years and the evidence of the past is everywhere: in place-names; in the traditions attached to rivers, rocks, caves; in cottages and manor houses, churches and taverns. Site by site, *Gothick Devon* builds up a picture of a very special county and its people and, through the half-world that is folklore, it takes us back through the ages to prehistoric times and maybe even beyond.

Lundy

Lynmouth

Ilfracombe

Doone
Country

Combe Martin

Woolacombe

Challacombe

Braunton

Shirwell

Barnstaple

Westward Ho!

Appledore

Swimbridge

Stoke

Bideford

Drewstone

Hartland

Weare Giffard

Great Torrington

East Worlington

Bradworthy

Shebbear

Lapford

Holemoor

Hatherleigh

Colebrooke

Luffincott

Okehampton

South
Tawton

Branscombe's Loaf
and Cheese

Belstone

South Zeal

Cranmere
Pool

Chagford

Lewtrenchard

Moretonhampstead

Lydford

Warren
House Inn

Jay's Grave

Lifton

Brentor

Postbridge

Hameldow
Tor

Mary Tavy

Crockern Tor

Bellever

Ilsingto

Tavistock

Princetown

Dartmeet

Widecombe
in the Moor

CORNWALL

Crazy Well Pool

Ashburton

Delverton

Childe's Tomb

Buckland Abbey

Sheeps Tor

Buckfastleigh

Dewerstone
Rock

Staverton

Dartington

Plymouth

Ringmore

Bigbury-on-Sea

Burgh Island

Thurlestone

Salcombe

SOMERSET

• Knowstone

• Rackenford Holcombe •
              Rogus
          Clayhidon•

Black Dog

      • Bickleigh

• Sandford   Membury •

                • Gittisham   DORSET

                • Ottery St Mary   Musbury
                                        •Uplyme
Ide • • Exeter   • Axmouth
                      Beer•
              Branscombe•
    Trusham East Budleigh • •Otterton
  •Hennock   •Exmouth
  •Chudleigh
Bovey Tracey

  Newton
  Abbot
Babbacombe •
  Torquay•
  Berry
  Pomeroy
Totnes
      • Brixham

  •Dartmouth

Stokenham

Gothick
DEVON

Places mentioned in the gazetteer

0   5   10 Miles

0   5   10   15 Kilometres

5

Long Strike haunts the lanes around Wortham Manor, Lifton, stepping from hedge to hedge.

Using this book

The numbers preceding the directions at the end of each entry are sheet numbers and grid references for Ordnance Survey Landranger maps. Place-names in bold type indicate cross-references.

Detailed opening times of properties can be obtained from *Historic Houses, Castles and Gardens Open to the Public* (British Leisure Publications, published annually); or for those belonging to the National Trust (NT) from the Devon Regional Office, Killerton House, Broadclyst, Exeter EX5 3LE (telephone: 0392 881691); or for English Heritage (EH) properties, from Bridge House, Clifton, Bristol BS8 4XA (telephone: 0272 734472). The abbreviation AM denotes an officially designated Ancient Monument.

Parts of the Devon countryside are used by the Ministry of Defence (MoD) as training areas. These are indicated in the text and are accessible outside live firing times. Live firing times are given in the local press (on Fridays for Dartmoor) and at local post offices, police stations, information centres, etc. For Dartmoor you can also ring the following numbers: Torquay (0803) 294592, Exeter (0392) 70164, Plymouth (0752) 701924, and Okehampton (0837) 52939.

A gazetteer of Gothick places

Appledore

Take off your shoes if you go past the Bloody Corner at night, otherwise the Dane, Biorn Ironside, will hear you. Another Dane, Hubba, is said to be buried under a flat rock in the quay called Wibblestone (i.e. Hubbastone). The Danes (Vikings) repeatedly invaded England during the second half of the ninth century and at the end of the tenth.

OS 180: ST 4630. 2 miles (4 km) north of Bideford on A386. Bloody Corner is a sharp bend just before Northam . A footpath runs through the quay (a shipyard) from Corner. **Westward Ho!** *is very near.*

Ashburton

Dawn't 'ee go down the riverzide:
Cutty Dyer du abide.
Cutty Dyer ain't no gude;
Cutty Dyer'll drink yer blood!

An ogre called Cutty Dyer lives in the river here, especially near North Street and at Cuddyford Cross. He lies in wait for drunkards and pulls them into the water.

OS 202: SX 7569. Cuddyford Cross, SX 758709, where the footpath crosses the road beside the stream; footpath from Great Bridge ($^1/_2$ mile or 800 metres). **Buckfastleigh** *is nearby.*

Axmouth

In the church is the fourteenth-century effigy of a priest with his feet on a dog. According to local lore, this was his favourite pet, whom he asked to be buried with him. In his will he left the church a piece of ground still known as Dog-acre Orchard.

OS 192 or 193: SY 2591. On B3172 1 mile (2 km) from Seaton. The effigy is in the north wall of the chancel; Dog-acre Orchard is now part of the churchyard. **Beer, Musbury** *and* **Uplyme** *are nearby.*

Babbacombe

In 1884 one of Babbacombe's most respected inhabitants, a Miss Keyse, was found murdered. Suspicion fell on John Lee, her manservant, and he was brought to the gallows in **Exeter**, but three times as he stood there the trapdoor stuck fast — although it worked perfectly when he was taken away. Eventually he was led back to prison, where he spent the next 23 years, always protesting his innocence. No one would live in Miss Keyse's house after the tragedy and it was eventually demolished in 1894.

Various explanations for the failure of the gallows have been put forward, including conspiracy, witchcraft, divine intervention, faulty mechanics, wet woodwork and drunken executioners.

OS 202: SX 920650. A suburb of Torquay. Miss Keyse's house was at the south end of the beach.

Barnstaple

No one knows when the town's ancient fair was first held. It starts on the Wednesday nearest 19th September and lasts for three days. Sophie Hancock, one of the fair's characters around 1900, was famous for being able to swear for half an hour without repeating herself. Each September she would appear before the magistrates and when fined would add a pound for the poor box.

Beware of your beer in North Devon

7

if there are frosts in May, particularly on the 19th, 20th and 21st. Local brewers promised to adulterate their beer if the Devil sent frosts to destroy the apple blossom of their rivals, the cidermakers. These three days are sometimes called St Frankin's Days, either after a brewer called Frankin or after the Devil himself.

*OS 180: SS 5533. **Braunton, Shirwell** and **Swimbridge** are easy drives away.*

Beer

Sixteenth-century Bovey manor house was a smuggling headquarters. There is supposed to have been a tunnel from the house down to the cliffs and a trapdoor in the roof for quick exits. A chamber was found in the well-shaft which was probably for the storage of contraband. In recent years, when repairs were being carried out, a secret room was also found in which there was an old chair. When this was removed poltergeist activity is said to have started, but as soon as the chair was replaced all was calm again. The house also has a priest's hole in the roof where persecuted Catholic clerics may have hidden.

Beer limestone has been quarried since Roman times and the labyrinthine Old Quarry was the perfect hiding place for smugglers. Parts of old casks and sailcloth that would have wrapped bales of silk and satin have been found in the passageways and legend has it that there is a tunnel down to the cliffs. There is also a secret chapel which was used by Catholics at the time of the Reformation. The entrance to the quarries is supposed to have been guarded by the ghost of a Roman centurion.

John Rattenbury, Devon's most famous smuggler and pirate, was born here in 1778. Numerous stories of his daring are told in his memoirs, probably ghost-written, which were published in 1837. On one occasion the press-gang cornered him in an inn but he took up a position behind a stable door with the bottom half closed, armed with a reaping hook and a knife. Here he held ten men at bay for four hours until some women managed to distract the officers by running in and pretending that there was a wreck on the beach and a young boy in danger of being drowned. Unlike most smugglers, who ended their days in poverty, having been in the pay of merchants during their careers, Rattenbury retired with a small pension from two local lords, one of them being Lord Rolle of Bovey House.

OS 192: SY 2389. 7 miles (11 km) from Sidmouth. Take A3052 towards Seaton and turn right on to B3174 at Hangman's Stone. Bovey House Hotel, SY 208902; turn right shortly after turning on to B3174. Quarry, SY 215895, in Quarry Lane; continue on down the road past Bovey House; guided tours Easter to end of October (telephone: 029780 282).

Bellever

A ruined cottage beside the East Dart river is known as Snaily House although its proper name is Whiteslade. The story goes that it was once inhabited by two women who always looked

John Rattenbury, the smuggler and pirate from Beer.

The stocks on Belstone green.

plump and well fed in spite of having no vegetables or animals to sustain them. Fearing witchcraft, the neighbours decided to search the house, where they found a pan of slugs and snails preserved in salt. Disgraced, the women pined away and died.

OS 191: SX 653773. Turn off B3212 at Postbridge. Snaily House (Whiteslade), SX 663763, 1 mile (1.5 km) on foot following the East Dart river southwards, on its east bank just past the hut circles. **Crockern Tor** *and* **Two Bridges** *are nearby.*

Belstone

On the village green there is a set of ancient granite stocks.

On Belstone Common is a prehistoric stone circle known as the Nine Maidens. Legend has it that the maidens were turned to stone for dancing on the sabbath but that they come to life again every day at noon. This can be seen 'only when conditions are favourable'. There are seventeen stones, although superstition has it that no two

counts are ever the same. Religious associations may account for the figure nine, and 'maiden' possibly derives from *maen*, the Cornish word for stone. The same story is attached to a stone circle at Stall Moor near Ivybridge and to many other groups of stones.

Dartmoor has many prehistoric stones. Their original purpose may be obscure but smaller circles like this one usually enclosed burial mounds.

OS 191: SX 6193. 2¹/₂ miles (4 km) from Okehampton off B3260. Nine Maidens (AM), SX 612928, on the left ³/₄ mile (1 km) on foot along the track past the inn. **South Tawton** *and* **South Zeal** *are nearby.*

Berry Pomeroy

The ruined Berry Pomeroy Castle is reputed to be one of the most haunted places in Devon, if not Britain. It is a sixteenth-century house within eleventh-century castle walls and was abandoned after being struck by lightning in 1685.

Berry Pomeroy

The ramparts at Berry Pomeroy Castle, walked by a white lady, and (right) the wishing tree in the grounds.

A beautiful lady in a rich blue dress has been seen in a large outer room and is said to be an omen of death (of someone nearby, not of the beholder). She is a Pomeroy daughter who had a child by her father which she strangled in an upstairs room.

Lady Margaret Pomeroy, dressed in white, walks the ramparts near St Margaret's Tower. She was imprisoned by her sister Eleanor as both loved the same man and Margaret was the more beautiful. Some say that she presages madness and death to the beholder, or that she lures people to destruction by a fall into a dungeon.

Another daughter of the house fell in love with the son of a rival family, whom she used to meet clandestinely in the castle grounds. One day her brother surprised the lovers together and stabbed them both to death. They are now seen reaching out to each other in vain.

There is a wishing tree which must be circled three times backwards, preferably blindfolded. The present tree was adopted in the 1970s as the original one was so old that it had rotted away.

Legend has it that at Pomeroy's Leap two sixteenth-century Pomeroy brothers blindfolded their horses and jumped over the precipice to their deaths rather than surrender to the king, having first hidden the family treasure somewhere in the castle. A young workman from Totnes called Jan Nokes dreamt on three consecutive nights that he would find treasure in one of the castle's fireplaces. On the third night he decided to go and look for the treasure and on his way he met

Sawbones, the local doctor, who advised him to go home and try in the morning. When Jan arrived at the castle the following morning he found that the fireplace had already been broken into and that there was no treasure. The doctor suddenly became very rich. This story was told in 1879 by a local who believed it to be true.

OS 202: SX 8261. Castle (EH) open Good Friday or 1st April to end of September; the exterior in winter by footpath from the road, ³/₄ mile (1 km). Turn left off A385, the Totnes to Paignton road, ¹/₂ mile (1 km) from Totnes, or right off A381, the Totnes to Newton Abbot road, 2 miles (3 km) from Totnes. The wishing tree is by the car park. Pomeroy's Leap is to the north (to the right from the main entrance). **Dartington, Staverton** *and* **Totnes** *are nearby.*

Bickleigh

The Carew family have lived at Bickleigh Castle since the early sixteenth century. Bampfylde Moore Carew, born in 1693, has been likened to Fielding's Tom Jones and nicknamed

Bampfylde Moore Carew from Bickleigh, the King of the Gypsies.

the King of the Gypsies or the King of the Beggars. He went to Blundell's School, the 'Eton of the West', but was forced to flee after hunting a tame deer for several hours through fields of standing corn. He fell in with a band of gypsies and took to earning a living by begging for charity at the houses of the rich, many of whom treated him rather like a court jester.

He used various ingenious disguises such as a shipwrecked seaman, a madman, someone whose house had burnt down, or — with a raw steak attached to his knee — a wounded soldier.

After winning a lottery he settled down to a more conventional life with his wife and daughter. He died in 1758 and is said to be buried in the village.

OS 192: SS 9407. On A396, 9 miles (15 km) from Exeter and 3 miles (5 km) from Tiverton. Bickleigh Castle, SS 936067, 1 mile (1.5 km) from village, signposted from A396; open Easter to early October, various afternoons (telephone: 08845 363). 'Old' Blundell's (NT), SS 9512, in Station Road, Tiverton; forecourt open.

Bideford

The first North American Indian to visit Britain is buried in Bideford churchyard. Brought here by Sir Richard Grenville from an island off the coast of Carolina in 1585, he was baptised in Bideford one year and died there the next.

The Devil is supposed to have disputed with the Virgin Mary over the siting of Bideford Bridge in the fourteenth century. He wanted it half a mile further upstream than she did and kept destroying the foundations put up by Mary and her followers. Eventually they sank large packs of wool at their chosen place and these became so weighed down with rubbish and mud that they were able to complete the bridge before the Devil could do anything to stop them. The idea of using the sacks of wool had come to the parish priest in a dream two nights running.

Bideford
OS 180: SS 4526. Bideford Bridge (AM), SS 455264. Appledore, Weare Giffard and Westward Ho! are nearby.

Bigbury-on-Sea

In 1900 children digging in the sand found a skull and several bones identified as belonging to a negro crew member of the *Chantiloupe*, stranded in the bay in 1772. Not only was the boat's cargo plundered, but a rich woman survivor was robbed and killed. According to a local newspaper 'the savage people from the adjacent villages...seized and stript her of her clothes, even cutting off some of her fingers, and mangling her ears in their impatience to secure the jewels, and left her miserably to perish'.

OS 202: SS 6544. 6 miles (10 km) south of Modbury. Take A379 towards Kingsbridge and then B3392. Burgh Island is opposite.

Black Dog

Named after Devon's ubiquitous

ghost, this hamlet is said to have been haunted during the Civil War by a hound which guarded the entrance to a tunnel running from an old well at the crossroads to Berry Castle earthworks.

OS 191: SS 8009. 11 miles (18 km) from Crediton via Morchard Bishop (Church Street). Berry Castle, SS 802093; turn at the crossroads to Sandford and Crediton and take a footpath on the right 1/3 mile (500 metres) along the road; the earthworks are past a farm 1/2 mile (1 km) away. East Worlington and Lapford are fairly near.

Bovey Tracey

At the time of the early Crusades the heiress of Parke manor fell in love with a knight who went away to fight. When she heard (wrongly) that he was dead, at her father's insistence she agreed to marry another. During the wedding the knight returned and scorned her, thinking she was faithless. In anguish she fled and stabbed herself to death. The knight decapitated his rival. Every

The beach at Bigbury-on-Sea.

The old well at Black Dog and (right) the tomb of the customs officer at Branscombe.

year in June, on the anniversary of the wedding, a white rabbit is seen running through the garden and a headless horseman gallops down the avenue of beech trees.

In the twelfth century Parke was acquired by William de Tracy, who gave the town its full name. Famous as one of the four knights who murdered Thomas à Becket, he is said to have built the church in penance, and then died on his way to the Holy Land, tearing his flesh with his teeth in a frenzy of remorse. That church has gone but pictures on the screen of the present church may relate to the story.

Letters from a Parliamentary chaplain tell how on 8th January 1646 Oliver Cromwell's men surprised a group of Royalist officers gambling in Front House, Fore Street. The officers diverted the soldiers by throwing their money out of the front window and escaped through the back of the house. (See also **Trusham**.) By the side of the footpath from Avenue Road to Challabrook is a cross commemorating a Royalist officer called Langstone, erected by the townspeople because of his kindness to them.

OS 191: SX 8178. On A382. The manor of Parke has gone and only the park remains

(NT). **Chudleigh, Hennock** *and* **Ilsington** *are nearby.*

Bradworthy

A seventeenth-century vicar, William Lang, was accused of insulting parishioners, extracting money by fraud, poisoning his predecessor's wife, conspiring to poison his predecessor, using the vicarage as a tavern, forgery and arson.

OS 190: SS 3213. 7 miles (11 km) north of Holsworthy by the minor road via Chilsworthy.

Branscombe

In spite of its romantic image , smuggling was a desperate business and it has been said that nearby **Beer** thrived as a centre of the illicit trade precisely because no customs officer dared set foot there. On a gravestone in the churchyard here is the following enigmatic inscription:

Here lieth the Body of Mr. John Hurley, Custom House Officer of this Parish. As He was endeavouring to extinguish some Fire made between Beer and Seaton as a Signal to a

Branscombe

Smuggling Boat then off at Sea He fell by some means or other from the Top of the Cliff to the Bottom by which He was unfortunately Killed. This unhappy Accident happened the 5th [9th?] Day of August in the Year of our Lord 1755. Aetatis suae 45. He was an active and Diligent Officer and very inoffensive in his life and Conversation.

OS 192: SY 1988. 5 miles (8 km) from Sidmouth off A3052 towards Seaton. The tomb is in the left-hand corner from the main entrance.

Branscombe's Loaf and Cheese

Walter Branscombe, whose tomb can still be seen in the cathedral, was Bishop of Exeter in the thirteenth century.

One day, when returning home across Dartmoor with his chaplain, he sat down for a rest on Sourton Common, whereupon a stranger appeared and offered him some bread and cheese. The Bishop was about to accept when the chaplain noticed that the stranger had cloven hooves instead of feet. Realising that this was none other than the Devil in disguise, the chaplain dashed away the food, which flew off to form two enormous rounded boulders, ever since known as Branscombe's Loaf and Cheese. The Slipper Stones to the south-east are the Bishop's shoes, which he had lost shortly before.

OS 191: SX 561892. A 3 mile (5 km) walk east across the moor from Sourton (on A386 between Lydford and Okehampton). Slipper Stones, SX 562887. Ministry of Defence training area (see page 6).

Braunton

The John and Lilley came ashore To feed the hungry and cloathe the poor.

The barque *John & Lilley*, with a cargo

Old White-hat haunts Braunton Burrows.

of cotton, silk, pots, pans, food, muskets and gunpowder, was wrecked on Saunton Sands in January 1843, having spent eleven days in distress out at sea. The crew, completely drunk after spending those eleven days in the liquor store, were given shelter for the night by the stalwart lighthouse keeper and his wife, but coastguards were unable to protect the boat from the hordes of looters who descended on to the beach. These included women as well as men, local farmers, and one man who was reputed to have brought a horse and cart down and gone away fully laden.

In December 1770 the *Juba* of Bristol, with a cargo of palm oil and elephants' tusks, was driven on to Saunton Sands and for many years afterwards during heavy storms tusks would turn up among the dunes.

Old White-hat or Jack the Whit-hat

haunts the south of Braunton Burrows wearing a big white hat with a lantern on it. Like the ghosts of **Woolacombe**, he tries to spin ropes of sand, but his main activity is hailing boats so that he can get a lift over to **Appledore**. If you go ashore to pick him up, you will never get away alive.

OS 180: SS 4836. 4 miles (6 km) from Barnstaple on A361. Access to Saunton Sands from Saunton on B3231. Part of Braunton Burrows, the sand dunes between Braunton and Saunton Sands, is a Ministry of Defence training area (see page 6). Woolacombe is fairly near.

Brentor

The thirteenth-century parish church is strikingly situated on a rocky promontory, believed to be part of a volcanic cone, with views to Dartmoor, Plymouth Sound, Cornwall and Exmoor. The Devil is supposed to have chosen the site and as fast as the stones were put in place down below he carried them back up again. When the

Brentor church was sited by the Devil.

church was eventually completed, St Michael, to whom the church is dedicated, got his own back by kicking the Devil down the hill, throwing after him a huge rock, which is still there.

When the church was restored in 1889-90, forty skeletons were found below the floor.

OS 201: SX 470804. Off A386, the Okehampton to Tavistock road. Lydford and Mary Tavy are nearby.

Brixham

Bob Elliott, a smuggler, made his headquarters in a cave in the cliffs of Berry Head. He was always known as Resurrection Bob because one day, when the coastguard came to search his cottage, his henchmen hid some brandy in a coffin and pretended Bob was inside it. The coastguard tactfully withdrew but was surprised to come across him in the lane that night carrying his own coffin.

In the town hall is a tablet commemorating the British warship *Formidable*,

The vampire's tomb at Buckfastleigh.

which was torpedoed on New Year's Day 1915. The dead numbered 648, but as many as 201 were saved, including one young seaman who was presumed dead and was laid out on the shore covered with sacking but was revived by the warmth of a dog which came to lie on top of him.

When the gardens of the Berry Head Hotel were being dug, a large number of human remains were found, now commemorated on a small stone inscribed 'To the unknown dead'.

*OS 202: SX 9255. **Dartmouth** is nearby.*

Buckfastleigh

At Brook Manor lived a Squire Richard Capel (or Cabell), a persecutor of village maidens, whom he would capture and keep locked up. He was also supposed to have been a vampire. To make sure he never troubled them again when he died, the villagers buried him with a heavy stone on his head inside a solid altar tomb inside a building with an iron grille, all of which can

still be seen in the churchyard opposite the church door. Do not be tempted to put your finger through the keyhole of his mausoleum as it is reputed he will bite it.

He died in 1677 and some say Dartmoor's phantom pack of black dogs, the Whisht Hounds, caused his death by chasing him across the moor until he dropped from exhaustion. Others say that as he lay dying the pack gathered round his house, baying horribly. Some also say that on a certain night early in July Capel rides his carriage up the drive to Brook Manor pursued by the hounds (and without his head).

These legends may have partly inspired Conan Doyle's story *The Hound of the Baskervilles*, which is set on Dartmoor.

The church was built on top of a hill above the town and as at Brentor there is a tradition that the site was chosen by the Devil. In July 1992 the church was gutted by a fire which had started at the altar.

In 1872 or 1873 at Buckfast Abbey, which was then in ruins, a boy out fishing saw a group of monks walking in single file through bushes near the river. As they wore grey or white they could have been Savigny or Cistercian monks from the twelfth century.

The hamlet of Deancombe is haunted by the weaver Thomas Knowles in the shape of a black dog. Knowles refused to hand over his business to his son, Phillip, even when dead and could be heard rattling away in his workshop all day long. The exasperated son Phillip called in the vicar, who threw a handful of churchyard earth in the phantom's face and turned him into a large black hound. This was then banished to Hound's Pool in the Dean Burn with orders to bale out the water with a perforated nutshell — which is why you can hear a strange grinding noise in the stream when it is full.

There is a phantom cottage, complete with occupants, which appears and disappears at dusk near Hayford, last reported in the 1890s.

OS 202: SX 7466. Brook Manor, SX 713677, 3 miles (5 km) north-west. The church is most easily reached by car by turning left at the top of the hill past the Abbey; on foot it is a ten-minute climb from the town. Buckfast Abbey (restored and used as a monastery), open daily all year (telephone: 0364 42519). Deancombe, SX 723643, 1 mile (2 km) south-west. Hayford, SX 6867, about 3 miles (5 km) west of the town. Ashburton, Dartington, Staverton and Totnes are nearby.

Buckland Abbey

Once a Cistercian monastery, the abbey became the home of Sir Francis Drake in 1581. In the museum is Drake's Drum, which plays whenever England is in danger. The drum's age and provenance were authenticated when it was offered in part payment for death duties in 1964. The legend seems to have arisen with a poem written by Henry Newbolt in 1885. Drake, a sea captain of humble origins who rose to defeat the mighty Spanish fleet, has long been credited with supernatural powers.

The drum is said to have been heard before the battle of Trafalgar (1805), on a West Country ship at Scapa Flow

Buckland Abbey is the home of Drake's Drum.

Buckland Abbey

when the German fleet surrendered at the end of the First World War, and on the Hampshire coast in September 1940.

*OS 201: SX 487667. NT/Plymouth City Council (AM). 11 miles (18 km) north of Plymouth. Turn off A386 just before Yelverton. **Tavistock** is nearby.*

Burgh Island

The island is connected to the mainland by a narrow causeway covered at high tide. The fourteenth-century Pilchard Inn is reputed to have been the hideout of Tom Crocker, the sixteenth-century 'prince of smugglers' and part-time pirate. There is a carving of him on one side of the fireplace and on the other is the mutilated face of an excise man. There is also a cave, only accessible from the sea, called Tom Crocker's Hole and Tom is said to walk the island every year in November.

The island was bought in the 1920s by the millionaire Archibald Nettlefold and the luxurious Art Deco hotel he built was the setting for Agatha Christie's detective novel *Evil Under the Sun*, 1941.

OS 202: SX 6443. By foot or sea tractor from Bigbury-on-Sea.

Chagford

In 1641, outside the Three Crowns inn just after her wedding, a girl called Mary Whiddon was shot dead by a jealous former suitor. The murder may have inspired a similar event in R. D. Blackmore's *Lorna Doone* (see **Doone Country**). A stone slab set into the floor of the church near the altar commemorates her with this verse:

Reader wouldst thou know who here is laid,
Behold a matron yet a maid.
A modest look, a pious heart,
A Mary for the better part.
But dry thine eyes, why wilt thou weep,
Such damselles do not die but sleep.

In 1971 a young man who was about to be married and was staying at Whiddon Park, the house where she had lived, saw a woman in black which was thought to be her ghost.

Burgh Island: the Pilchard Inn is the white building on the right.

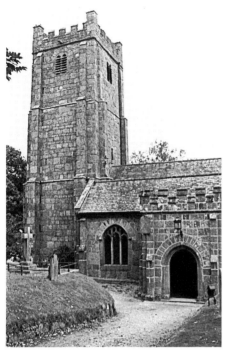

Chagford church and (right) the Three Crowns inn where a bride was murdered in the seventeenth century.

At Wonson Manor four men in Cavalier dress are occasionally seen playing cards in a downstairs room, and in one of the bedrooms a lady is felt smoothing the pillow of the bed and tucking in the occupant.

OS 191: SX 7087. Off A382 between Whiddon Down and Moretonhampstead. The church chancel is closed to the public. For Whiddon House turn left at Easton Cross, then first left. Wonson, SX 673896, 3 miles (5 km) by minor roads through Murchington; the manor (now a farm) is opposite the Northmore Arms pub.

Challacombe

This area of Exmoor is rich in bronze age burial barrows (also called cists or tumuli), few of which have escaped the attention of grave-robbers in spite of the dire consequences predicted for those disturbing antiquities (see also **Widecombe**).

A man who was excavating Broken Barrow for treasure some time before 1630 heard or saw phantom horses and was so shocked that he went deaf and blind and died soon afterwards. Fire-breathing dragons used to be seen at Chapman Barrows.

OS 180: SS 6941. Turn off A39 at Blackmoor Gate, between Barnstaple and Lynton, on to A399 (formerly B3226) and then left on to B3358. Broken Barrow (AM), SS 665417, on private land left of a track to the left shortly after turning on to B3358. Chapman Barrows (AM), SS 692454-700432, 2 miles (3 km) on foot left (north) from Barton Gate just before Challacombe, Combe Martin and Shirwell are nearby.

Childe's Tomb

Childe was a hunter caught in a blizzard on this lonely part of Dartmoor. He slaughtered his horse and huddled inside the still-warm carcass for protection, but his body was found frozen to death, apparently at the spot where his monument now stands. Nothing of the 'tomb' — rectangular granite blocks topped with a rough granite cross — is original, as the stones were taken for use in local buildings and the site was 'restored' at the end of the nineteenth century, but underneath is a prehistoric burial chamber or cist.

The story first appeared in print in Tristram Risdon's *Survey of Devon* (1605-30), but Risdon says that the original cross no longer existed and he did not specify whereabouts on the moor Childe died. Childe is thought to have been either a fourteenth-century landowner from Plymstock or a Saxon, his name deriving from the courtesy title 'cild', which would place him about six centuries earlier.

According to Risdon, the inscription on the original cross told that as he lay dying he wrote a will in his blood (or that of his horse) to the effect that whoever buried him should have his lands. History relates that monks from Tavistock were the first to arrive and, in order to avoid a rival party waiting at Tavy Bridge, constructed a second bridge further upstream now known as Guilebridge — but whether this is because of the monks' craftiness or because it leads to the Guildhall is open to debate.

OS 202: SX 626703. From the centre of Princetown take the minor road through Tor Royal towards Whiteworks (a disused tin mine) but stop at the leat (watercourse) just before. Follow the leat south until it goes into a tunnel and then continue south and east, leaving Foxtor Mires to your left (1 mile/2 km).

Chudleigh

A favourite rendezvous of Dartmoor's pixies is Chudleigh Rock, at the base of whose south face is a cave known as Pixies' Hole. Inside the cave have been found the bones of many prehistoric creatures such as sabre-toothed tigers, hyenas, bears, lynxes and rhinoceroses, but the reason it is now barred by a gate is the colony of rare bats which lives there.

Even in the nineteenth century mothers in the area would tie their babies to their cots to stop the pixies stealing them or swapping them with a pixy child. Some say that pixies are the souls of children who died unbaptised.

The Highwayman's Haunt inn is probably Rowell's Farm, where the highwayman Jack Withrington, who operated between Exeter and Ashburton, used to shelter. His four brothers were also highwaymen and all five were eventually hanged.

Dainton Lane, Chudleigh Knighton, is said to be haunted by a dwarf and if you manage to follow him he will lead you to a great treasure.

OS 191: SX 8679. Off A38 10 miles (16 km) south of Exeter. Chudleigh Rock, SX 8678, on left at the edge of the town just before next junction with A38. Open April to October, entrance through Rock Garden and Nursery. Inn on left after first turning off A38. Chudleigh Knighton, SX 8477, on B3344 towards Bovey Tracey. **Hennock, Newton Abbot** *and* **Trusham** *are nearby.*

Clayhidon

An iron plaque by the side of the road reads:

Wm Blackmore Landsurveyor, of Clayhidon Mills, was murdered, on this spot, the 6th day of February, 1853, by George Sparks of this parish, who was executed at Exeter for the horrid crime.

Blackmore had been collecting his fees and on his way home had talked to Sparks at an inn. Sparks followed Blackmore outside and attacked him

Chudleigh Rock is the home of pixies.

The Highwayman's Haunt inn (below) is on the road to Exeter from Chudleigh.

with a large pair of tongs.

OS 181: ST 1615. *Between Tiverton and Wellington (Somerset) via B3391 from Uffculme and minor roads through Culmstock and Hemyock. Plaque, ST 163141; from the village follow the road south; at a crossroads turn left and follow the road downhill; the plaque is after a bridge, on the right-hand side of the road just before the next crossroads.*

Colebrooke

One of Devon's most famous wrestlers, Abraham Cann, was born here in 1794. Unlike his gigantic rivals, such as the 23 stone (146 kg) James Polkinghorne from Cornwall, Abraham was a trim 5 feet 8^1/$_2$ inches (1.74 metres) but had surprising strength in his legs. He once boasted that in five minutes he could kick to rags the legs of his opponent. (See also **Mary Tavy**.)

Around about 1900 something that looked like a red monkey jumped out on a group of young men passing by and attacked one of them. He lashed out at it with a whip, whereupon it screamed like a child. It then followed them to the village, where it vanished. A few days later the creature appeared again and held out a bunch of flowers. One of the youths took hold of the flowers. He was dead within a week.

Crockern Tor was where the medieval tin miners held their court.

OS 191: SX 7799. 3 miles (5 km) from Crediton by minor roads. Turn left off A377 towards Copplestone. **Black Dog,** **Lapford** *and* **Sandford** *are nearby.*

Combe Martin

The seventeenth-century Pack o' Cards pub is supposed to have been built by a Squire Ley with money he won at cards. It has four floors — one for each suit — 52 steps in the staircase and 52 windows, although some were later blocked up to escape window tax. The inn used to have a table called the Press Gang Table, with a compartment where three men could hide when the press-gang raided, but this disappeared in 1988.

OS 180: SS 5846. The pub is on the Ilfracombe road. **Ilfracombe** *is nearby;* **Challacombe** *and* **Shirwell** *are fairly near.*

Cranmere Pool

The name of this boggy hollow in one of the bleaker and more remote areas of Dartmoor means 'lake of the crows'. It is haunted by Benjie Geare (Benjamin Gayer), a sixteenth-century mayor of Okehampton, who groans and wails at night and who appears in the shape of either a black pony or a black dwarf. He had been haunting the town so badly that a priest banished him to Cranmere with orders to empty the pool with a sieve. After several years' unsuccessful bailing Benjie killed a sheep and spread its skin across the sieve. He then emptied the pool so quickly that Okehampton was flooded and thirteen priests had to be called in, one of whom addressed him in Arabic and managed to turn him into a colt (or a dwarf).

OS 191: SX 603858. 5 miles (7 km) on foot across open moor from Bulworthy (SX 660865, near Chagford), or 7 miles (11 km) from Lydford. Ministry of Defence training area (see page 6).

Crazy Well Pool

This lonely pool is thought to be the result of surface tin mining and only 15 feet (4.5 metres) deep. However, in the 1930s a young man tried to touch the bottom but found himself sinking into a sort of pit whose walls closed in around him. An earlier story tells how villagers from nearby Walkhampton tied the church bellropes together and lowered them into the water but were unable to touch the bottom.

Legend has it that a voice from the pool, or a reflection in it, on Midsummer's eve will indicate the next person in the parish to die. It is said that two youths this century were challenged to spend Midsummer's Eve at the well. As they rode home later that night their motorcycle crashed and both were killed.

OS 202: SX 582705. Between Yelverton and Princetown. Turn right off B3212 ¾ mile (1 km) past Dousland, then take a left fork and follow the minor road for a further 1 mile (1.5 km) to Cross Gate. Then follow the footpath through the wood for 1½ miles (2 km). **Sheeps Tor** *is fairly near.*

Crockern Tor

Dartmoor's tors, with their fantastic shapes, look man-made but they were caused by weathering. Crockern Tor was considered the centre of Dartmoor by the moor's tinners and it was here that they held their own independent courts from probably the fifteenth century to the eighteenth. The granite table and seats they used had disappeared by the end of the eighteenth century, although the Judge's Chair may now be at Dunnabridge near **Dartmeet**.

Crockern, the spirit of the moor, rides a skeleton horse over the stones at night, rattling his bones. A rich Manchester man came to Dartmoor determined to enclose the land near Crockern Tor and start working it. According to the Reverend Sabine Baring-Gould in *A Book of the West* (1899), a man who lived in the area dreamed that Old Crockern, 'grey as granite, and his eyebrows hanging down over his glimmering eyes like sedge, and his eyes deep as peat water pools', was not at all happy about the Manchester man's plans and vowed: 'If he scratches my back, I'll tear out his pocket.' After many years of scratching the moor's

Dartington Hall, where the appearance of a white lady presages death.

23

back, and with his pocket empty, the man gave up and returned home.

OS 191: SX 615757. On the left of B3212 just beyond Two Bridges in the Postbridge direction. There is a footpath from Two Bridges. Dartmeet and Princetown are within easy reach.

Dartington

The present Hall was built in the fourteenth century but its history dates back to at least the ninth. In spite of its serene atmosphere, it is haunted by a white lady, who presages death, usually of a member of the Champernowne family, which lived here for nearly four hundred years from 1554 until 1925.

In 1890 she appeared to a maid three weeks before the death of Richard Champernowne, then rector of the church, and in 1897 a daughter of the family reported seeing her in a dream three weeks before her brother died in India. She was last seen in the 1920s by a postman and a maidservant on a moonlit night along the drive. The

postman died a few weeks later from the shock.

OS 202: SX 7862. 2 miles (3 km) from Totnes on A384. Gardens and Cider Press craft centre open to the public all year (telephone: 0803 864171). Hall (part AM), open for conferences, concerts and plays (telephone: 0803 862271). Berry Pomeroy, Staverton and Totnes are nearby.

Dartmeet

Just outside this hamlet, a short walk from the road, is the Coffin Stone, two granite slabs where bearers would rest coffins being taken for burial. The small crosses and initials they carved can still be seen.

There is an old belief that the river Dart claims one life a year and can be heard calling for its victim beforehand. At Rowbrook Farm there once worked a lad called Jan Coo. Over several months a voice was heard calling his name but no one could ever find the caller. One evening the voice seemed to come from over the river and, deter-

The Coffin Stone near Dartmeet.

Dewer hunts his pack of 'Whisht Hounds' across Dartmoor.

mined to find out who it was, Jan started to cross the river, stepping from boulder to boulder. His figure disappeared in the winter twilight and was never seen again.

At Dunnabridge Pound is an enormous granite seat which, according to tradition, was once the Judge's Chair at the medieval tin-mining courts at **Crockern Tor**. The pound itself is a remarkable remnant of the Bronze Age, covering ¹/₄ acre (0.1ha) with walls 5 feet (1.5 m) high and 3 feet (90 cm) thick.

*OS 191: SX 6773. 5 miles (7 km) from Two Bridges on the B3357. Coffin Stone, SX 679733, off the road leading to Ashburton to the right halfway up the hill; best located by taking small green track (not the main path) from the car park at the top of the hill. Rowbrook Farm, SX 686725, right off the road to Poundsgate. Dunnabridge Pound, SX 645746, on right 2¹/₂ miles (4 km) away on B3357 to Two Bridges, just after cattle grid. **Crockern Tor, Postbridge** and **Princetown** are nearby.*

Dartmouth

The Royal Naval College is haunted by Squire Boon, whose house used to occupy the same spot and whose daughter after his death married someone of whom he had disapproved. His ghost bargained that he would return to the grave if his daughter accompanied him and, while she kept her part of the bargain, dying three months later, he did not.

The town is haunted by a white rabbit and by Spring-heeled Jack, who leaps up on to rooftops rattling his chains.

In the church of St Saviour is the skull of Sir Charles McCarthy. Sir Charles had been killed by Ashanti forces in Sierra Leone, where he was governor, and the warriors had carried off his skull in triumph to use as decoration on their war drum. Six years later, in 1829, the skull was recaptured by British troops, brought back and buried with honours in the chancel.

*OS 202: SX 8751. **Brixham** and **Stokenham** are fairly near. Boat trips upriver to Totnes.*

Dewerstone Rock

This grim crag is home to Dartmoor's Devil figure, Dewer, who hunts over the moor with his pack of jet black 'whisht Hounds' ('whisht' being an old dialect word for 'eerie'). As late as the 1870s a coroner's jury recorded that a man found dead without any apparent cause was 'struck down by the phantom hunt'.

In the 1890s a groom at **Okehampton** reported hearing hounds at night when none would have been out and in this century a child near **Princetown** saw a pack of hounds which no one else could see.

The story is told of a north Dartmoor farmer who saw a pair of horns in a marsh and fled in terror thinking he had seen Dewer. When he and a band of men went to the spot next day they found a stag frozen to death in the ice. (See also **Buckfastleigh** and **Hameldown Tor**.)

25

OS 201: SX 538638. 7 miles (11 km) from
Plymouth, near Shaugh Prior, either off
A386 towards Tavistock or by minor roads
from Plympton. **Buckland Abbey** and
Yelverton are nearby.

Doone Country

R. D. Blackmore set his famous his-
torical romance *Lorna Doone* (1869) on
Exmoor, and Lank Combe, which bears
the most resemblance to the fictional
Doone Valley, is honoured with the
description 'Doone Country' on Ordnance Survey maps. The real
Badgworthy Water forms the bound-
ary between Devon and Somerset but
is not exactly the same as the fictional
one. Lorna Doone Farm at Malmsmead
claims to be one of the more probable
sites for Plover's Barrows Farm, the
home of the book's hero, Jan Ridd. (See
also **Lynmouth**.)

Blackmore was brought up in North
Devon and used legends of the area for
his fiction, which is set in the seventeenth century. One legend concerned
a band of outlaws called the Doones
supposed to have descended either from
a fugitive soldier from the battle of
Sedgemoor (1685) or from a Scottish aris-
tocrat (as Blackmore has it). The book's
dashing highwayman, Tom Faggus,
with his beautiful and intelligent mare,
comes straight from legend, as does the
wise woman, Mother Meldrum, whose
cave can be seen near Lynmouth.

Blackmore, like Jan Ridd, attended
Blundell's School at Tiverton (see
Bickleigh), which had a ferocious reputation as a fighting school, and where,
unlike his hero, he was severely bullied,
a possible cause of the epilepsy which
led him to give up his career as a barris-
ter and turn to writing.

OS 180: SS 7845. 2 miles (4 km) on foot
from Malmsmead, following the
Badgworthy Water. Malmsmead is 9 miles
(15 km) from Lynmouth off A39 towards
Minehead. Alternatively turn off A39 3
miles (5 km) from Lynton on to B3223 and
park after 2 miles (4 km) at the second

parking bay on the left; it is then a well-
signposted 2 mile (4 km) walk across open
moorland.

Drewstone

In the mid 1970s rumours began to
circulate of a puma-like creature living
wild in north-east Devon. Numerous
different people, usually local and often reputable, reported seeing a large
black long-tailed cat-like animal, about
4 feet (1.2 metres) long and 2 feet (60
cm) high. Other reports mentioned a
sand- or stone-coloured animal. In
spring 1983 a spate of sheep killings
around this hamlet brought both the
police and the Royal Marines to the
area to hunt for what was by then
known as the 'Beast of Exmoor'.

Although it is usually sighted in daylight, no one gets close enough to take
a clear photograph. Similar creatures
have been spotted in Cornwall and
Scotland and some naturalists believe
they are pumas, either escaped from
wildlife parks, or descended from pets
let loose after the 1976 Dangerous Animals Act.

OS 180: SS 742274. 3 miles (5 km) from
South Molton off B3227 towards Bampton.
Knowstone is fairly near.

East Budleigh

One of Devon's 'smuggling parsons'
was Ambrose Stapleton, who left his
signature, dated 1794, on a window
pane of the old vicarage, as did an earlier smuggling parson of the village,
Matt Mundy. Mundy's signature is
dated 24th September 1741.

OS 192: SY 0684. On B3176 between
Newton Poppleford and Budleigh
Salterton. 5 miles (8 km) from Exmouth.
Otterton is nearby.

East Worlington

A lone standing stone, called the

The Long Stone at East Worlington and (right) the Turk's Head at Exeter.

Long Stone, in a field near the village is said to have been dropped by the Devil when he heard the bells of the church.

OS 180: SS 774136. Turn left off B3137 at Gidley Cross between Tiverton and South Molton and then left at Burrow Cross. The stone, SS 778157, is on private land on the right after 1¹/₃ miles/2 km, before the village.

Exeter

The last woman in the county to be executed for witchcraft was Alice Molland, who was hanged here in 1684/5. The Rev Sabine Baring-Gould (1908) recounts the trial of three reputed witches in 1682. All were eventually hanged even though the only evidence against them was their confessions, which they later denied, and the testimony of two women who said they had given them 'pricking pains'.

For several miles beneath the city centre runs a network of aqueducts. Roman remains have been found, but the oldest vaulted passage dates from the time of the Black Death (mid fourteenth century), when masons would have had to contend not only with a 4 foot 6 inch (1.5 metre) high working space but also with swarms of plague-carrying rats. Although the passages have been enlarged for modern visitors, some members of most tour parties succumb to claustrophobia.

The Turk's Head inn in the High Street is said to be named after a Turkish prisoner executed in the cellars and whose head was then used as a target in the jousting ground behind the pub.

In the Cathedral, immediately to the right of the main entrance, is a memorial to R. D. Blackmore.

OS 192: SX 9292. Underground passages (AM), open throughout the year (telephone: 0392 265858); entrance off High Street. Ide is near.

27

Exmouth

On the night of 8th February 1855 someone or something left a trail of footprints in the snow from Teignmouth to Exmouth. Rather like a donkey's prints, they were cloven and travelled in a dead straight line, over rooftops and walls, under bushes, through outbuildings and a drainpipe and from one side of the frozen estuary to the other. 'The Devil's footprints' have never been satisfactorily explained. Apart from the Devil, a donkey, a racoon, an otter, a rat, a cat, a toad, a badger, a kangaroo, a great bustard, birds with iced-up feet and a swan from Germany carrying a donkey's shoe have all been credited with making the tracks.

In 1826 in the kitchen of Belmont House, Bicton Street, a cook saw the apparition of a headless child. Two weeks later, Fontelautus Dennis, aged about two, of the same address, died after a fall which injured his head. His head was removed for examination and his coffined body put in an attic room to await burial. For the next three days his mother and his favourite sister, Maria, heard his voice, in several different places and speaking sometimes for as long as half an hour, and Maria saw his hand reach through an opening between the attic and the staircase. People say the house is still haunted.

A sixteenth-century man from Littleham was persecuted by the ghost of his neighbour, which the parson proved unable to exorcise. The captain of a trading vessel anchored nearby suggested trying the new incense, tobacco, recently introduced by Raleigh. Sir Walter, who lived not far away at Dartmouth, duly taught the man how to smoke and the ghost 'departed, coughing and sneezing, to the tobacco-less world' (*A Book of the West* by S. Baring-Gould, 1899).

St John's church, Withycombe Raleigh, was abandoned in 1778 because of 'the crowds of spirits and bogles which frequented that desolate building and its adjoining cemetery'

Joanna Southcott, prophet or charlatan?

(1846). It was restored in 1926-37. Its bells ring of their own accord, it is said, when a lord of the manor of Withycombe dies, hence the rhyme:

The bell of Wythcombe they say
Spontaneous tells the fatal day.

OS 192: SY 0080. Bicton Street is off Rolle Street. St John's church is off St John's Road. **East Budleigh**, **Exeter** *and* **Otterton** *are fairly near.*

Gittisham

Britain's most famous prophetess, Joanna Southcott, was born here in 1750. From lowly beginnings she rose to great wealth and fame with her followers at one time numbering 144,000 and affecting special dress. At the age of 42 she had started to announce the imminent second coming of Jesus and to sell 'passports to paradise' and 'certificates for the millennium' — sealed prophecies to be opened in the year 2000. In 1814, at the age of 64, she claimed that she was about to give birth to the Messiah and that after her death she would rise again. Shortly afterwards, in December 1814, she died and was found to have been suffering from dropsy. She was buried in London.

Sixty years later, when her tomb was shattered by an explosion, people were still hoping for her return. In Bedford is kept a box of prophecies she left, which is supposed to contain the solution to the problems of the world; this has still been only partly investigated and a campaign continues for it to be opened. She herself was suspicious of the source of her inspiration and seems to have been self-deluded rather than a charlatan

OS 192: SY 1398. 2 miles (3 km) from Honiton off A30 towards Exeter. Ottery St Mary is nearby.

Great Torrington

Henry Lee, mayor of the town in the sixteenth century, took a major part in the 1549 Western Rebellion against the King. The rebellion failed and, thinking that all had been forgotten, the mayor was pleased to receive Sir Anthony Kingston, the King's Provost-Marshal, to dinner. When Sir Anthony arrived he asked the mayor to have the town's scaffold ready as he had an execution to perform later in the day. After the banquet the Provost-Marshal asked Lee to show him to the gallows, where a few minutes later Lee himself was hanged.

Devon's pixies love to confuse people and make them lose their way. In June 1890 a local newspaper printed a story about a man working in a wood outside the town who was kept on his hands and knees for five hours, not knowing who or where he was until he managed to crawl into a stream, where he recovered his senses. All around he heard peals of laughter. Water can help in such situations, as John Fitz found (see **Okehampton** and **Princetown**) but, as the paper pointed out, the usual remedy against pixies is to turn your pockets inside out.

*OS 180: SS 4919. **Bideford** and **Weare Giffard** are nearby.*

Hameldown Tor

Dewer, Dartmoor's demon huntsman, hunts the souls of babies who have died unbaptised (see also **Dewerstone Rock**). A man riding home one night was startled by the sound of a hunting horn and a pack of jet-black hounds with glowing eyes which swept past him. When a huntsman came into view the man asked him what he had caught that day. Laughing, the huntsman threw him the bag, telling the man to keep it. When the man got home he unwrapped the bundle and found inside it not some tasty small animal or bird but instead the dead body of his own child.

OS 191: SX 7080. Turn left off B3212 at Challacombe Cross 8 miles (13 km) from Moretonhampstead in the Princetown direction and follow the road for 1¹/₂ miles (2 km). Continue on foot east (left) to Grimspound Prehistoric Settlement (¹/₂ mile/1 km); the Tor is then south-east (right).

Hartland

The Cornish wrecker and smuggler Daniel (or David) 'Cruel' Coppinger lived here between 1792 and 1802 and his marriage is recorded in the church registers. One of the chief hiding places of his booty is supposed to have been in the cliff at Sandhole.

The swish of silk dresses thought to belong to two lady ghosts has been heard near Bow Bridge and in 1934 beautiful globes of soft white light were seen. These were 1¹/₂ to 2 feet (45-60 cm) in diameter, appeared for at least a minute at a time and rose to a height of 20-30 feet (6-9 metres). (Similar globes have more recently appeared in East Devon to a farmer on a tractor.)

Docton Bridge is believed to be haunted by a calf. Until at least the

The Hartland 'globes' appeared in 1934.

beginning of the twentieth century locals would not go near the bridge at night for fear of meeting the phantom.

OS 190: SS 2624. 13 miles (20 km) west of Bideford on A39 and then B3248. Sandhole Cliff, SS 220208, reached by minor roads via Philham, Edistone, Docton and Elmscott (8-10 miles, 13-16 km). Bow Bridge, SS 246247, on the road to Stoke. Docton Bridge, SS 245212.

Hatherleigh

At dawn on about the second Saturday in November a sledge of blazing tar barrels is dragged through the streets at breakneck speed, preceded by a bellringer to frighten away evil spirits. Various other festivities take place throughout the day, culminating in the evening in a carnival procession lit by flaming torches. In past years barrels were rolled instead of being dragged, a far more dangerous proceeding, and effigies of local miscreants were carried through the streets and then burnt. No one knows the origins of the carnival nor how far back it dates.

OS 191: SS 5404. 8 miles (13 km) from

Okehampton on A386 towards Great Torrington. Dates may vary depending on other local events. Holemoor, Shebbear and Winkleigh are fairly near.

Hennock

In Bottor Rock is hidden the treasure of John Cann, a Royalist who took refuge here for several days but was eventually tracked down by bloodhounds and hanged by the Parliamentarians. A blue flame hovers over the treasure's hiding place.

In 1957 it was reported that there had been three bicycle accidents on the road between Hennock village and Pitt Hill caused by a figure which ran alongside waving its arms up and down. The same figure has appeared on the A38 near **Chudleigh** and Stover.

OS 191: SX 8380. 4 miles (7 km) from Chudleigh. Turn left off B3193 at Lyneham. Bottor Rock, SX 826805; on private land on the right before a wooded area, 10 minutes walk along a footpath from Cherry Combe Head crossroads beyond the village. Bovey Tracey and Trusham are nearby.

Holcombe Rogus

In 1858 the Bluett family left Holcombe Court after four hundred years. The new owners kept hearing the faint crying of a child and when they were having the porch renovated the skeletons of a young woman and child were found. These were given a Christian burial and the crying stopped. It turned out that John Bluett, who had lived in the house two centuries before, had shut his mistress and her baby in a tower room and starved them to death so that he could marry a wealthy lady.

OS 181: ST 0519. 12 miles (20 km) from Tiverton. Take A361 and then A38 towards Wellington (Somerset); turn off and go through Burlescombe and Westleigh. Alternatively (and more tortuously), turn

The inhabitants of Ide erected the memorial above to their village, bisected by a main road. The twisted oak in the village (right) is supposed to have entrapped a troublesome spirit.

off B3227 between Bampton and Wiveliscombe (Somerset).

Holemoor

A man was killed by a trailing branch of a tree at the junction with Bovacott private road, and sounds of the accident are said to recur at night from time to time.

OS 190: SS 4205. Between Holsworthy and Hatherleigh off A3072. Bovacott junction, SS 423047, is the first junction on a smaller and steeper road from the village back to A3072. Shebbear is nearby.

Ide

In 1974 this lovely village was sliced in two by the A30 and one half became officially a suburb of Exeter. The villagers

erected a memorial tablet which reads as follows:

Remember that for many hundred years this was a beautiful valley where people could make their way to Ide through green fields and by the side of a running brook. It was destroyed in 1974 by the Department of the Environment
Geoffrey Rippon MP
John Peyton MP
Kieth [sic] Speed MP
Brigadier Baldwin.
Resolve that your generation shall leave England a more beautiful place than they found it and undo the vandalism of ours.

In the lost half of the village in the centre of a road junction is an oak tree

Ide

Jay's Grave on Dartmoor.

with a twisted trunk. Apparently this is because of a troublesome spirit trapped inside it. The spirit was such a nuisance, turning milk and beer sour, stopping dough from rising, frightening young women and making neighbours quarrel, that an Oxford scholar was called in to lay it. Some say that the spirit belongs to a Major James Pitman, who committed suicide in 1848, since the tree twisted the night he died. Nearby is the Twisted Oak pub.

OS 192: SX 8990. 2 miles (3 km) from Exeter off B3212 to Moretonhampstead. For the pub turn left before the village. The tree is up the road to the left of the pub and the memorial is to the right of the pub in the private field just before the footbridge over A30.

Ilfracombe

One of the earliest records of a wreck is on a tombstone in the parish church. This is dated 31st October 1635 and reads: 'Bryant Tooker and two Frenchmen, parte

of a shipps companie called ye *John*, were drowned at our harbour mouth'.

Gold and silver coins, thought to come from a Spanish ship returning from the West Indies with slaves in the late eighteenth or early nineteenth century, still turn up from time to time in the shingle of the harbour at low water. Smugglers, and perhaps even wreckers, are said to have used Chambercombe Manor as their headquarters. There is supposed to be a tunnel from the house to Hele Bay and in the nineteenth century a woman's skeleton was discovered in a sealed room. This is thought to have belonged either to a Spanish girl stripped of her jewellery after her boat was lured ashore by wreckers or to Kate Oatway, the daughter of the wreckers' leader, left there to starve by her own father. Lady Jane Grey (1537-54) also lived there.

OS 180: SS 5147. Chambercombe Manor, on the Watermouth Road (A399) towards Combe Martin; guided tours Easter to end of October (not Saturdays); gardens free; (tele-

phone: 0271 862624). Hele Bay, SS 536480, is on the left ½ mile (1 km) further on.

Ilsington

A phantom cottage has been seen on three different occasions in the twentieth century in broad daylight (unlike the Hayford apparition at **Buckfastleigh**) in woods here. It disappears before it can be reached and no old foundations have been found at the spot.

OS 191: SX 7876. Take B3387 from Bovey Tracey and turn left after 3 miles (5 km). Widecombe in the Moor is fairly near.

Jay's Grave

This wayside grave is always decorated with a pot of fresh flowers, a custom probably started by the Dartmoor writer Beatrice Chase, but she died in 1955 and no one admits to replenishing the pot today. It seems that Mary Jay was brought up in Newton Abbot workhouse at the beginning of the nineteenth century and then apprenticed at Ford Farm, Manaton, where she committed suicide when she was about sixteen, most probably because she was pregnant. Her grave was unmarked until 1860, when a roadmender came across some bones which were identified as belonging to a young woman. His wife remembered being told about Mary Jay and so the bones were placed in a wooden box and reburied. A mound was raised and the present stones were put in place.

OS 191: SX 732798. 2 miles (3 km) from Manaton, 3 miles (5 km) from Widecombe and 3 miles (5 km) from Beetor Cross; where a footpath crosses the road.

Knowstone

Devon used to be famous for its 'hunting parsons', one of whom was John Froude, vicar here from 1803 to 1852. Unlike the much respected Jack

Russell of **Swimbridge**, Froude was an evil man. Not only did he have a vicious tongue but he also kept a gang of thugs at his house to force tithes out of unwilling villagers. When Bishop Phillpotts of Exeter tried to visit him, his carriage sank into a pit that had been filled with peat by Froude's men, and when he wrote asking how many candidates Froude had for confirmation the reply, scrawled on the back of a list of hounds ill with distemper, was that none had reached the required standard — they could not say the Lord's Prayer backwards. Froude now haunts nearby **Rackenford**.

OS 181: SS 8223. 10 miles (16 km) from South Molton via B3227 in the Bampton direction. Drewstone is fairly near.

Lapford

Hidden round the back of the east end of the church is the grave of John (Jack) Arundel Radford, vicar here

The gravestone of Lapford's notorious vicar John Radford.

Lapford

Lewtrenchard Manor.

from 1825 to 1861, whose cross had to be cemented in place because his wickedness caused it to slew. (It is now the only cross in the graveyard *not* slewed.) He is said to emerge from a hole in the grave at night and travel to the old rectory. Radford terrorised his parishioners, ran up debts — forcing one tradesman to eat his bill between two slices of bread — and fathered innumerable illegitimate children. A curate sent to replace him was found with his throat cut and, although tried for the murder, Radford was acquitted for lack of proof and reinstated as parson.

The ghost of Thomas à Becket — 'Our Tom' — is supposed to ride round the church in a hat at midnight on 7th July. As at **Bovey Tracey**, the church was restored as a penance by William de Tracy, one of Becket's murderers.

*OS 191: SS 7308. 8 miles (13 km) from Crediton, on A377 towards Barnstaple. Black Dog, Colebrooke and Sandford are nearby. **East Worlington** is fairly near.*

Lewtrenchard

Lewtrenchard Manor was at one time owned by Margaret Gould, a woman of strong character who died in 1795. It is said that when she died all the shutters of the house flew open and a servant saw her standing by a walnut tree. Seven days later she was seen sitting on a plough dressed in white satin with her long hair down around her shoulders. In another story 'Madam' appeared to a woman who was stealing apples from the orchard and barred her way until she had emptied all her pockets. She is also said to be seen by a stream near the house dressed in white with a phosphorescent glow coming from her face and clothing.

When her tomb was opened by a carpenter in 1832 she is supposed to have sat up, got out of her coffin and chased the man home, giving off so much light that he could see his own shadow before him. It took seven clergymen to control the spirit, which they turned into a white owl. This now flits about outside the Manor.

The writer Sabine Baring-Gould (1834-1924) was a descendant of hers and vicar here for many years, living at the Manor. On one occasion, when one of Baring-Gould's children was ill, the

34

nurse heard a voice reminding her that it was time to give the child its medicine. In 1877 Baring-Gould and a friend heard footsteps and the sound of a silk dress but could see nothing and in 1918 two nurses gave notice because they saw the figure of a woman walking about the nursery and stooping over the children's beds. In 1967 a five-year-old child may have met Madam in the gallery.

OS 201: SX 4586. 11 miles (17 km) from Okehampton just off A30 to Launceston (Cornwall). Lewtrenchard Manor is now a hotel. Lifton is nearby.

Lifton

At night the lanes around Wortham Manor are haunted by a long-legged ghost called Long Strike who strides along the lanes and steps from hedge to hedge.

OS 201: SX 3885. On A30 15 miles (24 km) from Okehampton in the Launceston (Cornwall) direction. Wortham Manor, SX 382869, 1¹/2 miles (2 km) away by minor roads towards Yeat and Cross Green. Lewtrenchard is nearby.

Luffincott

Franke (*sic*) Parker, vicar here from 1835 to 1880/3, appeared in the rectory in ghostly form to a successor, Thomas Brown, who immediately fled the house and never went back. No one would live in the house after that and it eventually fell into ruin and disappeared. Parker collected rare old books (which are now in the Philpotts Library at Truro in Cornwall) and the story has grown up that he was involved in black magic and was able to turn himself into a lion, snake or wolf.

OS 190: SX 3394. 9 miles (14 km) from Holsworthy off A388 to Launceston (Cornwall).

Lundy

This island was probably used by the Vikings during their raids in the Bristol Channel, and from the twelfth century it was occupied by the Marisco family, Norman pirate-knights. William de Marisco was hanged and quartered in 1238 for attempting to assassinate Henry III. Only the foundations of the family's castle can still be seen, the building having been supplanted by Henry III in the thirteenth century with the castle that now stands above the landing beach.

During the Civil War Lundy was held by the Royalists and in the seventeenth century it was taken over by Algerian pirates.

Thomas Benson, Member of Parliament for Barnstaple from 1747 to 1749, used the island for smuggling, with the help of convicts he was meant to be exporting to the colonies. The authori-

The vicar of Luffincott was supposed to be able to turn himself into a lion.

ties finally caught up with him after he had deliberately scuttled a boat and made off with the insurance money. He fled to Portugal, where, rumour has it, he entered the priesthood. Benson's Cave below Marisco Castle is said to have been constructed by Benson with convict labour and used by him for hiding contraband.

The island has always been dangerous to shipping and Charles Kingsley made it the scene for the wreck of the Spanish galleon in *Westward Ho!* (1855). Jenny's Cove on the west coast is named after a ship lost in February 1797, homeward bound from West Africa with ivory and gold dust.

On 29th May 1906 the first-class twin-screw battleship HMS *Montagu* struck the Great Shutter Rock off the south of the island in fog. Unusually, the Navy directed salvage operations, which were lengthy and not very successful. When the Navy withdrew, the professional salvagemen had a party to celebrate. The ship's remains are still there underwater off rocks called the Montagu Steps.

The Devil has lent his name to some of the island's impressive volcanic features such as the Devil's Slide (north-west coast), the Devil's Chimney (half-way down the west coast) and the Devil's Limekiln (south-west tip), a huge cone 150 feet (46 metres) across at the top, 370 feet (113 metres) deep and tapering at the bottom to a tunnel which leads through to the sea.

OS 180: SS 1443. No cars allowed but the island is only 3 miles (5 km) long by ½ mile (1 km) wide. Sea passage from Bideford all year round (telephone: 0237 470422 or 477676) and from Ilfracombe in summer (telephone: 0271 63001). National Trust but administered by Landmark Trust (telephone: 0628 825925). Castle foundations in Bull's Paradise.

Lydford

At one end of the extraordinary Lydford Gorge, 1¹/₂ miles (2.5 km) long

and with vertical walls of rock in places 60 feet (180 metres) high, is the Devil's Cauldron, a deep pothole filled with swirling water, reached along a narrow path cut out of the rock face. It is signposted 'Unsuitable for those of nervous disposition'. In the seventeenth century the gorge harboured a clan of thieves and vagabonds called the Gubbins, who terrorised the neighbourhood and were portrayed by Charles Kingsley in his novel *Westward Ho!*

The gorge is notorious for suicides, including a Captain Williams who tried to spur his horse over Lydford Bridge but eventually had to dismount and jump, having first thrown the saddle and bridle over in order to disguise his intentions. These were found next day entangled in branches and led villagers to discover his body on the rocks below.

Kit's Steps, further up the river Lyd, are said to be haunted by an old lady – Kit? – in a red headscarf who slipped and fell to her death one evening on her way home from market. The name may, however, be derived from 'skit', meaning broken rock.

Lydford Castle was described in a 1512 Act of Parliament as 'one of the most hainous, contagious and detestable places in the realm'. The dungeon, for people who offended against the moor's tin-mining laws, was reached through a trapdoor and was completely windowless.

Until the thirteenth century all Dartmoor's dead had to be buried at Lydford and the route taken by the funeral processions was called the Lich (or Lych) Way, 'lich' being an old word for 'corpse'.

OS 191: SX 5084. Off A386, the Okehampton to Tavistock road. Gorge (NT), open all year (but a limited section in winter). Bridge (AM), at the main entrance to the Gorge. Kit's Steps, on private land, SX 516845, footpath from village. Castle (EH), open any reasonable time. Lich Way is marked on the OS map. **Brentor** *and* **Mary Tavy** *are nearby.* **Branscombe's Loaf and Cheese** *is fairly near.*

Lydford Bridge and (right) the interior of Lydford Castle.

Lynmouth

On the night of 12th January 1899 news came that a ship called the *Forrest Hall* was in distress off Porlock, 12 miles (19 km) away in Somerset. The sea was so rough, however, that the lifeboat could not be launched from Lynmouth but the villagers succeeded in saving the ship by taking the 8 ton lifeboat by road to Porlock and launching it there. Twenty horses and every able-bodied man, woman and child were recruited for the journey, which took eleven hours and included negotiating a 1 in 4 hill and digging away the bank in some places to widen the road.

Disaster struck the village on the night of 15th August 1952 when 90 million tons of water from the East and West Lyn rivers cascaded on to it, sweeping all before. 34 people died or went missing and much of the village was destroyed. Help poured in from all over the world but it took four weeks before the village could be re-opened. Many people were presented with medals for bravery, a Flood Memorial Building was erected and at the foot of Countisbury Hill is a plaque to Robert Carnegie, who directed the relief work, the rebuilding of the village and subsequent engineering works to prevent anything similar from ever happening again.

R. D. Blackmore is supposed to have written much of *Lorna Doone* (see **Doone Country**) while staying at the Rising Sun Hotel in the nineteenth century. The Valley of the Rocks nearby, with its rocks eroded into fantastic shapes, has a cave named after a legendary local wise woman, Mother

Lynmouth

Meldrum, who appears in the novel.

OS 180: SS 7249. *Valley of the Rocks, SS 705494, 1 mile (1.5 km) west of the village by road or footpath; the cave is at the western end of valley, south of the road.* Challacombe *and* Doone Country *are fairly near.*

Mary Tavy

Fixed to the outside of the church is a memorial to John Hawkins, a blacksmith, who died in 1721. It reads:

Here buried were some years before,
His two wives and five children more:
One Thomas named, whose fate was such
To lose his life by wrestling much.
Which may a warning be to all
How they into such pastimes fall.

Wrestling was a favourite sport in the West Country until the nineteenth century and several Devon men became nationally famous (see **Colebrooke**). Whereas the Cornish specialised in

'hugging and heaving', Devonians went in for 'kicking and tripping', the toes of their boots hardened with blood and fire.

OS 191: SX 5079. *On A386 4 miles (6 km) from Tavistock in the Okehampton direction. Memorial on the south wall of the chancel.* Brentor *and* Lydford *are nearby.*

Membury

In an unmarked grave in the churchyard are the remains of an old woman called Hannah Henley (or Anley), who was buried in 1841 and is still remembered as a witch. Not only could she put spells on people and animals but she could also remove weeds from a field. Everyone was frightened of her and a local farmer called in a white witch from Somerset. Hannah started to waste away and one morning she was found lying in the stream outside the cottage with a kettle she had been trying to fill. The villagers set fire to her cottage, leaving only a few stone foundations intact. It is said no crops will

Blackingstone Rock, Moretonhampstead, where King Arthur fought the Devil.

The effigies of the Drake family in Musbury church are said to come to life at midnight.

grow in the field where her cottage stood, known ever since as Witches Field.

OS 193: ST 2703. 8 miles (12 km) from Axminster. Take A358 to Chard and then turn left. Musbury is nearby.

Moretonhampstead

The remains of a cairn on Mardon Down are known as the Giant's Grave or Maximajor's Grave. Nearby is a 6 foot (2 metre) high pillar, possibly a prehistoric standing stone, called the Maximajor Stone or Headless Cross. The two are remembered in the following rhyme:

Underneath this great tall stone
Maximajor lies
And, if you goes at twelve at night,
You'll hear most awful cries

The Devil and King Arthur had a fight and the stones they threw at each other formed all the rock piles in the area, including Blackingstone Rock. After winning the fight, the Devil went to Northlew near **Hatherleigh,** where he died of cold

(and is said to be buried in the churchyard, just inside the lych-gate).

An old moor story tells of a woman who left her baby behind to go to the fair. She later found the baby's remains—a heap of well-picked bones — in a raven's nest on the top of Blackingstone Rock.

OS 191: SX 7586. Maximajor's Grave SX 767874, left off B3212 at Cossick Cross, 3 miles (5 km) towards Exeter; after about a mile (1.5 km) it is a short walk to the left, Blackingstone Rock, SX 786855, is signposted right at Cossick Cross. Chagford is nearby.

Musbury

In the church is an ornate tomb of members of the Drake family between 1558 and 1643. It incorporates statues of three couples which are said to rise from their knees at midnight and walk across the churchyard to a nearby stream. There they have a drink and then they return to the church.

OS 193: SY 2794. Between Seaton and Axminster off A358. Axmouth and Uplyme are nearby.

Newton Abbot

In Bradley Woods is an enormous hollow in the ground, a collapsed limestone cavern, known as Puritans' Pit after William Yeo, parson of Wolborough, who preached there when he was deprived of his living for refusing to acknowledge Church of England laws after the Restoration.

Above the door of tiny, thirteenth-century Haccombe church are one horseshoe and a piece of another. These belonged in the sixteenth century to a member of the Carew family from Haccombe House who wagered with Sir Arthur Champernowne of **Dartington** Hall that his Devonshire roan horse could swim further out into Torbay than Sir Arthur's Barbary courser. Carew not only won but rescued his opponent as well and he nailed up his four horseshoes as thanks. A poem about the wager, written by an Exeter schoolmaster in the early nineteenth century, is also pinned to the door.

*OS 202: SX 8671. Puritans' Pit, SX 844709. Take the public footpath right off A381 to Totnes, opposite Bradley Road. Follow it for twenty to thirty minutes, leaving the river on your right, until past Bradley Manor. Haccombe church, SX 8970; interior open Wednesday afternoons April to October, exterior at any time; turn off A380 towards Combeinteignhead and turn right in Netherton. **Babbacombe**, and **Chudleigh** are nearby.*

Okehampton

Lady Howard's Walk in the extensive ruins of the eleventh-century castle is named after the phantom from **Tavistock** who arrives each night in the shape of a black dog. Like other troublesome ghosts (for example see **Cranmere Pool, Woolacombe**) she has a hopeless task to keep her out of mischief, in her case to strip the grass bare — but only one blade a night.

To the south of the town is Fitz's Well, marked by a cross said to have been erected by John Fitz (see **Tavistock**) in the sixteenth century after being pixy-led on the moor — the same story as that attached to Fice's Well at **Princetown**.

*OS 191: SX 5895. Castle, EH (telephone: 0837 52844); 1/2 mile (1 km) outside the town. Fitz's Well (AM), SX 592938; 2 miles (3 km) away, on the right of the road leading to Okehampton Camp. **Belstone**, **South Zeal** and **South Tawton** are all nearby.*

Otterton

A local man who killed his wife when drunk was condemned to be hanged on a common near the village but instead he was put in a cage and left to starve, with watchers being paid to ensure no one gave him food or drink. The fees paid to the watchers still appear in the churchwarden's accounts.

*OS 192: SY 0785. Off B3176 between Newton Poppleford and Budleigh Salterton. **East Budleigh** and **Exmouth** are nearby.*

Okehampton Castle is said to be visited nightly by a black dog ghost.

40

Fitz's Well (right), near Okehampton, yields water that is proof against pixies.

Ottery St Mary

The town's tar-barrel rolling each 5th November has been described as 'one of the most alarming experiences life has to offer short of all-out war' (Brian Shuel in *The National Trust Guide to Traditional Customs of Britain*, 1985) and draws vast crowds. Women and children, as well as men, hoist on to their shoulders huge barrels shooting with flames and career through the crowds at breakneck pace. Most fire festivals today have been restricted for safety (see **Hatherleigh**) but Ottery's has hardly changed since the eighteenth century, when it started.

In the north aisle of the church is a statue of a Captain Coke, supposedly murdered by his brother in 1632. The captain is said to get down at midnight and run around (see also **Musbury**).

OS 192: SY 0995. Tar-barrel rolling from about 8.30 pm. Gittisham is very near.

Plymouth

Until the seventeenth century there were two huge figures called Gog and Magog carved into the turf of the Hoe. These were said to commemorate a fight between Corineus, a Trojan who landed with Brutus (see **Totnes**), and Gogmagog, a resident giant, in which Gogmagog was hurled into the sea. The older figure, however, may have dated from the iron age. They are thought to have been covered by the Citadel, the fortress built by Charles II (1630-85).

Devil's Point is where the Devil took a leap to reach Cornwall but fell in when he heard that the county was full of saints. The strong tides and whirlpools of the strait are the result of his dipping.

On the Hoe is a statue of Devon's greatest hero, Sir Francis Drake (1540-96), who lived at nearby **Buckland Abbey**. It is said that the Devil helped him conjure up the storm that battered and dispersed the Spanish Armada. Another time he was whittling a stick on Devil's Point and as the shavings fell into the sea they became fully rigged ships. Nelson was thought by some to be a reincarnation of Drake, who will return whenever England needs him.

In 1591 a young woman called Eulalia Page, who lived in the city, was burned alive for conspiring to murder her husband (this was the penalty for petty treason, which included murder of a husband). She had been forced to marry a rich elderly man and after bearing him one stillborn child had shut herself in her room. She was sentenced by her uncle, and her father, later to be a judge himself, was also present at the trial. It is said he never smiled again after her death. There is a monument to him (Judge Glanville) in **Tavistock** church.

Samuel Reynolds, father of the painter Sir Joshua (1723-92), taught at Plympton grammar school and was a keen follower of astrology. The stars predicted that great danger would threaten the life of one of his children in its fifth year and so he ordered that the child should be kept indoors throughout that time. Notwithstanding his precautions, the child was accidentally dropped to its death from an upper window by its nurse.

In 1774 a Mr Day, a millwright from Suffolk, built a 'submarine vessel' in which he claimed he would stay submerged at 20 fathoms (120 feet or 37 metres) for twelve hours. On 20th June, carrying a hammock, watch, small wax taper, a bottle of water and two ship's biscuits, he entered the vessel, which was then towed out to a position north of Drake's Island and sunk. Crowds thronged the foreshore and bets were laid as to his success or otherwise. Neither he nor his vessel was ever seen again.

On the Barbican is a plaque to West country convicts who joined the first fleet bound for Botany Bay in Australia in 1787.

In 1796 an explosion during a farewell party aboard the warship *Amphion* killed about three hundred people, mostly local men, women and children. The deck was red with blood and covered with human remains, which had to be collected and taken to Stonehouse

naval hospital for identification. A gunner said to be stealing powder was blamed and during salvage a sack of gunpowder was found hidden in the ship's biscuits.

OS 201: SX 4755. Hoe, SX 4753, on the cliff area to the south of the city. The Citadel is used by the army, official tours only. Devil's Point, SX 459534, near Stonehouse and the Hoe. Plympton, northeast, off A38 towards Exeter. Drake's Island, SX 466528, opposite the Hoe. Barbican, in the quay area to the east of the Hoe. Dewerstone Rock and Yelverton are nearby.

Postbridge

The tortuous B3212 follows the route of one of the ancient tracks which cross the moor. In 1921 three accidents occurred on the road at Bellever Forest. In the first, a motorcycle swerved, the engine flew off and the driver was killed. In the second a coach mounted the bank and a passenger was seriously injured, and in the third a young army officer came off his motorcycle. In both the last two cases the drivers said they had felt as if invisible hands were gripping their own and pulling the vehicles over.

In 1924 a woman camped with her family at Powder Mills, a ruined nine-

A mortar standing near the isolated Powder Mills, a former gunpowder factory on Dartmoor.

The prison at Princetown.

teenth-century gunpowder factory, woke in the middle of the night and saw a large 'hairy hand' clawing at the window. It disappeared when she made the sign of the cross.

On the road northwards is a crossroads with the eerie name of the Watching Place. Horses rear here as if a ghostly hand clutches at their bridles. It is the site of the last gibbet to remain on the moor and beside it is Beetor Cross, one of the medieval crosses which marked out the trackways.

A procession of white-robed monks was seen in the twentieth century emerging from the lower end of Wistman's Wood. They faded away at the river ford below.

This ancient copse of lichen-covered, stunted oaks is also said to be one of the favourite haunts of the Whisht Hounds (see **Dewerstone Rock**), the name 'Whisht' perhaps deriving from the same source as the name of the wood.

OS 191: SX 646788. On B3212 between Moretonhampstead and Princetown. Bellever Forest stretches along B3212 from Postbridge to Powder Mills. Powder Mills (part AM, part a pottery open to public), SX 628769, 2 miles (3 km) away on B3212

towards Princetown. The Watching Place (Beetor Cross on map) SX 712841, 5 miles (8 km) back towards Moretonhampstead. Wistman's Wood (Site of Special Scientific Interest — please skirt), SX 6177, a 2 mile (3 km) walk west from Powder Mills. Crockern Tor is nearby.

Princetown

Dartmoor's famous jail was built here at the beginning of the nineteenth century to house French prisoners from the Napoleonic Wars. The prisoners fought so many duels that local court staff went on strike for higher pay because of the extra work they had to do. The prisoners also busied themselves with forging English money, gambling and stealing from each other.

American prisoners from the War of 1812 planned a tunnel 20 feet (6 metres) deep and 250 feet (80 metres) long but were betrayed by one of their number, who received his freedom and a passport in return. During a supposed riot among the Americans in March 1815 seven of them were killed, seven had to have an arm or a leg amputated and a further 53 were wounded. From eye-witness accounts it now appears that

Princetown

The sixteenth-century Fice's Well near Princetown.

the governor panicked because he found a small hole in a wall, ordered the six thousand or so restless prisoners back to their cells and then commanded his troops to fire on the prisoners as they struggled to get through the one small doorway.

When alterations were made to the town's church at the beginning of the twentieth century, many of the graves of French prisoners who had died in the jail were found to be empty. It is

presumed that the corpses had been sold in Plymouth for the use of medical students as there was a thriving trade in bodies during the Napoleonic Wars, the usual source, executed criminals, not being adequate for the number of doctors needing to be trained at that time (see also **Stoke**).

Fice's Well near the prison is thought to have been built either by John Fitz senior of **Tavistock** or by someone called John or James Fice. The lintel is carved with the initials I[J]F and the date 1568. The story goes that Fitz or Fice and his wife became hopelessly lost — pixy-led — when out riding on the moor but were restored when they drank from the stream here. They built the well in gratitude. The same story is told about Fitz's Well at **Okehampton**.

OS 191: SX 5873. In the middle of Dartmoor, reached by either B3212 or B3357. Fice's Well (AM), SX 577759; take B3357 towards Tavistock, turn right at Rundlestone and it is then a fifteen-minute walk along the first public footpath on the left. Bellever, Crockern Tor and Dartmeet are nearby.

The Stag Inn at Rackenford.

44

Rackenford

The thirteenth-century Stag Inn is haunted by the highwayman Tom King, an associate of Dick Turpin. The two men met and joined forces in1736, when Turpin tried to hold up King. Although King taught Turpin to conduct robberies in the manner of a gentleman, this did not diminish the violence and viciousness of their behaviour, which Turpin had learned as a member of the notorious 'Essex gang'. King is supposed to have been shot accidentally by Turpin when a party of police and irate locals discovered the outlaws' headquarters in Epping Forest. How Tom King arrived at the Devon inn is not known, but there may be confusion with Tom Faggus, Exmoor's bandit (see **Doone Country**).

According to local legend King did not die when shot by Turpin but lived to be hanged at Gibbett's Moor near here. His figure has been seen several times in the twentieth century in the pub and horses' hooves have been heard in the restaurant, which is built over a well.

The ghost of Parson Froude from nearby **Knowstone** gallops through the village.

OS 181: SS 8418. 7 miles (11 km) from Tiverton via B3137 and then Calverleigh. Gibbett's Moor, SS 8817, 4 miles (6 km) away on the road back to Tiverton.

Ringmore

In the tower of the parish church is a room with a fireplace, where the vicar, William Lane, hid for three months during the Civil War after a party of Roundheads had been despatched to capture him because he had led his parishioners into battle for the King. After the war Lane set out to walk to London to try to regain favour with the authorities, but he died on the way in 1654 and is buried in Alphington church, Exeter.

Ringmore church.

*OS 202: SX 6545. 5 miles (8 km) from Modbury. Take A379 towards Kingsbridge, then turn right on to B3392 and then right again at St Ann's Chapel. **Bigbury-on-Sea** and **Burgh Island** are very near.*

Salcombe

One of the best known wrecks of the twentieth century was that of the Finnish tall ship *Herzogin Cecilie*, which hit the Ham Stone at 4 am on 25th April 1936 and then grounded in Soar Mill Cove, where it was stuck for seven weeks. About one million people came from all parts of Britain to see the stranded vessel, causing so much congestion that special police had to be drafted in and farmers turned their fields into paying car parks. Eventually the ship was towed to Starehole Bay so that the cargo could be salvaged but this was by now so waterlogged that it had to be abandoned, as was the ship, which gradually broke up over the next three years and sank from view.

OS 202: SX 7338. Starehole Bay, SX 7236. Soar Mill Cove, SX 6937; 1½ miles (2 km) and 3 miles (5 km) respectively by South Devon Coast Path from Sharpitor. From Soar, SX 710379, Soar Mill Cove is ½ mile (1 km) on foot.

Sandford

On a pillar in the church is a fifteenth-century sculpture of two children tearing each other's hair out. This represents an incident in 1125(?) when two men, perhaps rabbit-catchers in dispute over their territories, came to blows during a service and one killed the other. Because of this the church had to be closed. In 1136 King Stephen visited Exeter and the villagers were able to persuade him to intercede with the bishop so that worship was resumed in about 1137.

*OS 191: SS 8202. 2 miles (4 km) north of Crediton. The pillar is left, halfway down the aisle. **Black Dog, Colebrooke** and **Lapford** are fairly near.*

Shebbear

On the green outside the church is a boulder weighing about a ton and measuring 6 by 4 by 2 feet (2 by 1 by 0.6 metres), which has come to be known as the Devil's Stone (and which has given its name to the village pub). Every 5th November at 8 pm, so as to ensure good luck for the village for the following year, the village bellringers have to toll the church bells and then turn the stone over.

The bellringing keeps evil spirits at bay but the significance of the stone-turning has been lost and no one knows how old the custom is. In wassailing, an age-old custom once practised in West Country orchards around the New Year, evil spirits were also frightened away, with the shooting of guns and the beating of pots and pans, so as to ensure a good crop of apples in the months ahead.

The nearest place the rock could have come from is Wales but according to one legend the Devil dropped the stone here during his descent from heaven. Another story is that the stone was intended for the foundations of Henscott church nearby but it vanished one night and reappeared in Shebbear. Every time it was rolled back to Henscott it returned to its present spot.

*OS 190: SS 4309. 9 miles (15 km) from Holsworthy. Take A3072 towards Hatherleigh and turn left at Brandis Corner. **Bradworthy** and **Great Torrington** are fairly near.*

Sheeps Tor

On the village side of this tor between two upright rocks among the boulders is a cave known as the Pixies' Cave where a Royalist is supposed to have hidden during the Civil War. There is room for two or three people inside and if you do go in you must avert the pixies' mischief by leaving them a small offering such as a pin or a piece of cloth (for their dressmaking). Some say that if you put your ear to the granite of tors you can hear the ringing of pixey bells.

*OS 202: SX 566682. Sheepstor village is 5 miles (8 km) from Yelverton. Take B3212 towards Princetown and turn right at Dousland after about 2 miles (3 km). The tor is about ¾ mile (1 km) from the village on foot. **Buckland Abbey, Crazy Well Pool** and **Dewerstone Rock** are all fairly near.*

Shirwell

A ghost of a man with a calf's head appears at the crossroads 1 mile (1.5 km) away at midnight. It is said to be that of a herdsman who was driving his cattle across the road and was knocked down by a horse-drawn vehicle.

OS 180: SS 5937. 5 miles (8 km) from Barnstaple off A39 towards Lynton. Crossroads, SS 590378; at the second turning to Shirwell off A39 from Barnstaple.

South Tawton

In the church are memorials to the Oxenham family who lived in the parish from the thirteenth century to the nineteenth. There was a tradition that the death of any member of the family would be heralded by a white or white-breasted bird. There are written accounts of sightings from the seventeenth century onwards, many of them by apparently reliable witnesses such as doctors and clergymen. One of the most dramatic instances concerns Margaret Oxenham, whose father saw a white bird hovering over her head during the feast on her wedding eve. The next day in church a rejected suitor stabbed her to death.

Just before the First World War neighbours of Amyas Oxenham in Exeter say they saw a white dove fly in through his bedroom window shortly before his death. Amyas's son went to live in Canada and there are even reports that the bird was seen across the Atlantic. The direct family line is now extinct.

OS 191: SX 6594. 4 miles (6 km) east of Okehampton. Either take B3260 from Okehampton and go through Sticklepath, or turn off A30 at Whiddon Down and go through South Zeal. Belstone is also nearby.

South Zeal

A wall of the room behind the bar in the twelfth-century Oxenham Arms Hotel is built around a standing stone which has its base buried deep beneath the floor. There is also reputed to be a tunnel between the inn and Oxenham Manor in **South Tawton**.

South of the village is Raybarrow Pool, which is not a pool, but one of the most

The Oxenham Arms in South Zeal.

dangerous bogs on Dartmoor. One day a man walking along the path which skirts it saw a hat on the ground. Lifting the hat, he was astonished to see a man's head underneath. 'What on earth are you doing?' he asked. 'What do you think I'm doing!' came the strangled reply, 'Sitting on my blooming horse, that's what.'

OS 191: SX 6593. 5 miles (8 km) east of Okehampton. Either take B3260 from Okehampton and go through Sticklepath, or turn off A30 at Whiddon Down. Raybarrow Pool, SX 6390; 3 miles (5 km) on foot. South Tawton and Belstone are nearby.

Staverton

The river Dart has a cruel reputation (see also **Dartmeet**). In August 1840 John Edmunds was married at Staverton church but within hours both he and his wife were swept away by a huge torrent of water from the flooding river. His wife's body was discovered almost immediately but his was not found for almost three weeks, and his horse was swept along for several miles.

OS 202: SX 7964. 4 miles (7 km) from Totnes, either via Dartington and A384, or off A381 towards Newton Abbot at Littlehempston. Berry Pomeroy is also nearby.

Stoke

In 1830 four men and two women were transported for digging up most of the graves in the churchyard and shipping the corpses out for anatomical studies. In the house where they lived were found cupboards and drawers stacked with teeth, also destined for sale.

In general body-snatchers preferred fresh corpses and these, without teeth, could fetch as much as twelve guineas each, or even twenty if they were in exceptional condition. Many an unclaimed body — from a wreck perhaps — was carried off by someone pretending to be a relative since parishes were only too anxious to avoid burial expenses.

OS 190: SS 2324. 2 miles (3 km) from Hartland by minor road.

Stokenham

A stained glass window in the south transept of the church commemorates 38 people who drowned in 1866. They came from the barque *Spirit of the Ocean* which was blown on to a submerged rock north of Start Point. There were four survivors, two of whom owed their lives to a gallant farmer who climbed down sheer cliffs to rescue them.

OS 202: SX 8042. On A379 5 miles (8 km) from Kingsbridge in the direction of Dartmouth.

Swimbridge

The most famous of Devon's 'hunting parsons' was Jack Russell, born in 1796, who has given his name not just to the village pub but also to the breed of fox terrier descended from his own pet, Trump.

His vigour was legendary. At the age of 79, it is said, he spent all week hunting, rode 70 miles (100 km) home on the Saturday afternoon, arriving at midnight, slept soundly and rose to conduct three services. On another occasion he fought bare-handed with a stag which had gored a parishioner 'muddled with cider'. Another story tells of his advertisement for a curate in which he stipulated that the man must be of 'moderate and orthodox views', which, knowing their vicar, the villagers presumed meant someone who could ride well.

He was respected for his preaching as well as his hunting and over a thousand people attended his funeral in 1883.

OS 180: SS 6230. 4 miles (6 km) from Barnstaple via Landkey by minor roads.

Tavistock

My Ladye hath a sable coach
With horses two and four.
My Ladye hath a gaunt blood-hound
That goeth on before.
My Ladye's coach hath nodding plumes;
The driver hath no head.
My Ladye is an ashen white
As one that long is dead.

Lady Howard, born Mary Fitz in 1596, about whom the above verse was written (taken from *Songs of the West*, 1895, by Sabine Baring-Gould), is said to run in the shape of a hound from the gateway of Fitzford House (all that remains of the family's home) to **Okehampton** Castle every night between midnight and cockcrow and to return with a single blade of grass in her mouth. In another version of the story she travels in a coach of bones, or in a black coach driven by a headless coachman and preceded by a fire-breathing black hound.

She is condemned to these actions because of crimes she is supposed to have committed, but no one knows what they are. She was, however, a forceful woman, four times married, beautiful and rich. It was her father, John Fitz, who was the criminal. Having murdered one of his acquaintances over some land, he then killed an inn-keeper when on his way to stand trial for the first murder, wounded the inn-keeper's wife, stabbed himself and bled to death. Her grandfather, on the other hand, also John Fitz, is remembered as the founder of two sacred wells, at **Princetown** and **Okehampton**. He died in 1589/90 and there is a memorial to him and his wife in Tavistock church.

The ninth-century abbey, of which only the tower remains, was said to have been founded by a Saxon giant, Ordulph, and his father, Orgar. Ordulph was so big that he could stand astride a river 10 feet (3 metres) wide and so strong that he once broke the bars of **Exeter** city gates with his bare hands when he found them locked. The tower is called Betsy Grimbal's Tower after a woman supposed to have been killed by a soldier on the spiral stairs. Stains said to be her blood can be seen there but Mr Bray, vicar here in the 1830s, said that they were more likely to be the effect of damp on the ironstone. She herself appears at a window of the tower before national disasters and a policeman claimed to have seen her in 1966 before the Aberfan tragedy.

In Grammerby Wood a ghost fires shots at you and if you look back as you leave you will see a Georgian gamekeeper. Luckily no one seems to get hit.

It used to be a tradition in the town on Midsummer Eve to look into the church through the keyhole to see the

Betsy Grimbal's Tower in Tavistock.

spirits of those to die — presumably during the coming year — walk into the church from the opposite doorway. The story goes that at the end of the eighteenth century two brothers saw themselves and both died very shortly afterwards.

The town suffered its worst epidemic of plague in the seventeenth century. Inside Merrivale stone circle, and others, the moor people left provisions for infectious townspeople, who left money there in return.

*OS 201: SX 4774. Abbey (AM) in Plymouth Road. Merrivale 4 miles (6 km) away on B3357; stone circle, SX553746, through the village, on the right. **Brentor** is nearby.*

Thurlestone

In January 1750 a Dutch ship laden with wine, brandy, coffee and indigo was wrecked on Thurlestone Sands. By the Saturday two days later as many as

Thurlestone_

The grave of drowned seamen in Thurlestone churchyard.

ten thousand people had congregated around the wreck intent on stealing the cargo. Soldiers were brought in from **Plymouth** and the leader of the crowd 'fell on one of the soldier's bayonets' and was killed.

Buried in the churchyard north of the tower are six sailors and a young boy thought to have come from the brigantine *Crossowen*. This was discovered on Yarmer Sands on 7th May 1908 without any crew but with all the sails set and only a small amount of water in the hold. It is thought she may have hit Burgh Island in fog and been abandoned.

OS 202: SX 6742. 3 miles (5 km) from Kingsbridge. Take A381 towards Salcombe and then turn right.

Torquay

At Petit Tor, St Marychurch, lanterns were placed at night on the horns of cows grazing in clifftop fields in order to confuse ships; this is one of the rare stories of deliberate wrecking in the county. Drake's Hole, a hollow in the cliffs at Petit Tor Beach, is named after a smuggler who lived in a cottage there.

Lady Cary, who was a great socialite in the 1770s, is still seen out and about at Torre Abbey. In the 1870s two young women saw her dressed in a ball-gown and riding in her carriage, which gave out a brilliant light.

OS 202: SX 9164. Petit Tor, SX 927662, near the Model Village. Torre Abbey (AM), near the sea-front; open April to October daily, gardens open all year (telephone: 0803 293593). Babbacombe is in Torquay.

Totnes

A lump of granite embedded in the pavement just above 51 Fore Street is known as the Brutus Stone. According to the twelfth-century historian Geoffrey of Monmouth, Brutus was a Roman of Trojan descent who sailed the western seas to seek his fortune. In 1171 he landed on the coast near Totnes, where he conquered the resident giants and named the land Britain after himself. According to legend it was the stone he first set foot on and said, 'Here I stand and here I rest, and this good town shall be called Totnes'.

Apart from the fact that the stone is several miles from the sea, Geoffrey's description of the area does not really tally and it seems that the name Totnes might have been used for the whole of the south-west coast. The name of the stone may be a corruption of 'brodestone' (great stone), the stone having been a waymark for travellers before the tenth century when Totnes grew up as a town.

From the twelfth century to the seventeenth a large leper hospital existed in Magdalen Road. The three sacred springs called the Leech Wells which used to be visited by inmates can still be seen. Leechwell Lane, once enclosed

50

Torre Abbey, haunted by Lady Cary, and (right) the Brutus Stone in Fore Street, Totnes.

between high walls for most of its length, is part of the route taken by the lepers from the hospital to the church via the wells.

Among the grisly remains in the six-teenth-century Guildhall, a prison for over 250 years, are stocks, a mortician's tap, truncheons and a bull-baiting post. The townspeople's enthusiasm for this sport continued long after it was shunned elsewhere in Britain, particu-larly on 5th November, when they would have two sessions, one before church and one afterwards. Specially bred dogs would attack tethered bulls and bring them to their knees ready for slaughtering. This was considered to make their flesh more tender. The prac-tice was outlawed in 1835.

OS 202: SX 8060. Guildhall off Fore Street above the Brutus Stone; open Easter to October. The Leech Wells are off Leechwell Lane off Leechwell Street near the Kingsbridge Inn. Boat trips to Dartmouth. **Berry Pomeroy** *and* **Dartington** *are nearby.*

Trusham

In the church is a memorial to John Stooke which mentions a charity he set up for the church and the poor of nearby Bovey Tracey. The story, first recorded in 1709, goes that in 1646 an officer in the Royalist army was gam-bling at Bovey when he was cornered by Roundheads. He threw his bag of winnings to his servant, who threw them over a hedge, where they were found by Stooke, then a humble farm-er's boy. Stooke's fortune was founded on his lucky find. Bovey's altar fund still receives a small yearly sum from the charity.

A 'black patch' has been reported in the parish and if you come across it you feel as if you are running into something solid.

In one of the houses something de-scribed as a 'shining golden glory' would sometimes come out of a cupboard. This cupboard was always very damp. The partition which formed the cupboard was removed in the 1930s and nothing unusual has been reported since.

Warren House Inn.

OS 191: SX 8582. 3 miles (5 km) north of Chudleigh either by B3193 or by minor roads. **Hennock** is nearby.

Uplyme

A black dog ghost used to visit a farmer here every night and sit next to the fire opposite him. One day the farmer chased him away, the dog made a leap for the ceiling, the farmer struck up at the dog and made a hole in the plaster, and out fell a quantity of Charles I coins. With the money he built the Black Dog Hotel and until recently Haye Lane behind the pub was called Dog Lane.

In 1856 the dog was reported in the lane at dusk, growing to enormous proportions and then vanishing. In 1959 a young couple visiting the area with their ten-year-old son were horrified one evening when the figure of a dog

appeared at eye level out of the hedge and floated across the lane into the hedge opposite. It is said that locals still will not venture into the lane at night and that the name was changed in an attempt to bury the legend.

OS 193: SY 3293. On the outskirts of Lyme Regis (Dorset). Turn off A3052 4 miles (7 km) from Seaton or off A35 2 miles (3 km) from Axminster. **Axmouth** and **Musbury** are nearby.

Warren House Inn

This, the third highest inn in England, is home to the classic Dartmoor tale 'Salting down Feyther', in which a traveller staying overnight in the inn is warned that he will have to share his room with 'Feyther'. Not understanding the dialect, he is horrified to find a corpse in his room. 'But I warned you about Feyther,' says the landlord. 'The snow being so thick, when old Feyther died two weeks ago we couldn't carry him to Tavistock to bury him and so Mother put him in the old box and salted him in — Mother's a fine hand at salting in.'

Merripit Hill nearby is haunted by a starving sow and her litter of piglets, who travel backwards and forwards to Cator in search of food.

Beneath Birch Tor opposite are medieval walled enclosures which look like playing-card symbols. These have been nicknamed 'Jan Reynolds' Cards' after a local scoundrel who is said to have dropped them while being carried off by the Devil for playing cards in **Widecombe** church.

OS 191: SX 673809. On B3212 2 miles (3 km) from Postbridge in the direction of Moretonhampstead. Merripit Hill, SX 657803, on the right back towards Postbridge behind a hut circle. Cator, SX 670770, over the road 2-3 miles (4 km) on foot south-east through Soussons Down Wood. Jan Reynolds' Cards best seen from the footpath from the car park opposite the inn. **Crockern Tor** is nearby.

Weare Giffard

The spirit of a thirteenth-century Sir Walter Giffard, who is thought to be buried in the church, is reputed to be restless because he was not buried with his wife. His ghost leaves the manor house, enters the churchyard by the lich-gate, goes into the church porch, knocks at the door and vanishes inside.

OS 180: SS 4721. Off A386 between Bideford and Great Torrington.

Westward Ho!

Occasionally the timbers of an unidentified Dutch East Indiaman wrecked in 1771 become uncovered on the beach and the ship's complete outline can be seen.

Pieces of a German schooner wrecked in 1926 still lie below the cliffs to the south of the beach. According to a newspaper report at the time, locals 'behaved in the most disgraceful manner, pillaging all they could lay their hands on, even personal photographs'. In 1800 a Bideford merchant called

Chanter put up a tower here from which to watch for the return of ships in which he had a financial interest. However, the first time he used it he saw his son's ship wrecked and 'Chanter's Folly' was abandoned, fell into ruin and was finally demolished in 1952.

OS 180: SS 4329. 1 mile (2 km) from Bideford. The South West Coast Path takes you along the cliffs south of the beach. Appledore is very near.

Widecombe in the Moor

On Sunday 21st October 1638, during a service, the church tower was struck by lightning and a lightning ball entered the church. Four people and a dog were killed and over sixty were injured. On a board in the church is a poem about the catastrophe, written at the time by the village schoolmaster. According to legend, the storm was caused by the Devil, coming to collect the soul of one Jan Reynolds, who had sold it to him for money to carry on his gambling. Jan's 'cards' can still be seen near the **Warren House Inn**.

Part of the 'lightning poem' in the church at Widecombe in the Moor, which recalls the catastrophe in 1638.

One man had money in his purse,which melted was in part,
A key likewise which hung thereto.and yet the purse no hurt,
Save only some black holes.so small as with a needle made.
Lightning some say,no scabberd hurts.but breaks & melts y blade
One man there was sat on the bier,which stood fast by the wall,
The bier was tore with stones that fell.he had no harm at all:
Not knowing how he thence came forth.nor how y bier was torn.
Thus in this doleful accident.great numbers were forborne.
Amongst the rest a little child which scarce knew good from ill.
Was seen to walk amidst the church.and yet preserved still:
The greatest admiration was.that most men should be free.
Among so many dangers here.which we did hear and see.
The church within so filled was with timber stones and fire,
That scarce a vacant place was seen.in church or in the choir:
Nor had we memory to strive.from those things to be gone,
Which would have been but work in vain.all was so quickly done.

53

Widecombe in the Moor

In spite of the taboo on tampering with antiquities (see also **Challacombe**), a former parson opened a local cist. The following night his house was destroyed by an explosion.

A phantom horseman rides the road from Cold East Cross to Hemsworthy Gate. In the 1950s he was seen at dusk wearing a military-style mackintosh with the collar turned up.

OS 191: SX 7176. 7 miles (11 km) west of Bovey Tracey on B3387. Cist SX 734755; take the track right off the road from Hemsworthy Gate to Cold East Cross; the cist is on the right after ½ mile (1 km). Cold East Cross, SX 741742; Hemsworthy Gate, SX 742761; the road is a right turning 2 miles (3 km) back along B3387 towards Bovey Tracey. Dartmeet is fairly near.

Winkleigh

In September 1975 at West Chapple Farm the bodies were found of two brothers and a sister, the remnants of a family who had farmed the area since the fourteenth century. The police concluded that Alan Luxton, the younger brother, had killed himself and that the older brother, Robbie, had killed first his sister, Frances, and then himself. No one knows the reasons for the tragedy as the family had become increasingly reclusive, but in his book *Earth to Earth* (1982), John Cornwell draws a compelling picture of the background to the tragedy (see Further reading).

OS 191: SS 6308. On B3220 8 miles (13 km) from A377 between Copplestone and Lapford. Hatherleigh is fairly near.

Woolacombe

The weird of the Tracys
That have always the wind and
the rain in their faces.

William de Tracy, from the family that owned the manor here, was one of Thomas à Becket's murderers in 1170, and because of this his descendants are forever doomed to gallop in a frenzy up and down the 2 mile (3 km) long sandy beach on stormy nights, wailing. William himself has the awful task of spinning ropes of sand which are then snapped by a huge black dog with a ball of fire in its mouth. (See also **Bovey Tracey**.)

OS 180: SS 4543. On A3123 (B3343). Turn off A361 at Mullacott Cross 2 miles (3 km) from Ilfracombe towards Braunton.

Yelverton

Black ghosts appear in many parts of the country and Devon in particular (see **Black Dog, Dewerstone Rock, Uplyme**), often along boundaries and roads. One such, which attacks people on the B3212 north-east of here and the A386 south, is said to be re-enacting the time he and his master were set upon and killed by thugs.

In the nineteenth century a man walking this route was accompanied by a strange dog but when he bent down to pat it his hand passed right through. The next morning he was found unconscious in a ditch.

OS 201: SX 5267. On A386 between Tavistock and Plymouth. Buckland Abbey, Dewerstone Rock and Princetown are nearby.

Further reading

Baring-Gould, Sabine. *Devonshire Characters and Strange Events*. John Lane, The Bodley Head, London, 1908.

Behenna, John. *Westcountry Shipwrecks*. David & Charles, Newton Abbot, 1974.

Brown, Theo. *Devon Ghosts*. Jarrold, Norwich, 1982.

Clay, Emily. *Extraordinary Parsons of Devon and Cornwall*. Devon Books, Exeter, 1986.

Cornwell, John. *Earth to Earth: The True Story of the Lives and Violent Deaths of a Devon Farming Family*. Allen Lane/Penguin, London, 1982.

Crossing, William. *Guide to Dartmoor*. 1912. Reprinted, Peninsula Press, Newton Abbot, 1990.

Devon Folklife Register. *Shades and Spectres*. Exeter City Museums Service, 1980.

Household, G. A. (editor). *The Devil's Footprints: The Great Devon Mystery of 1855*. Devon Books, Exeter, 1985.

Larn, Richard. *Devon Shipwrecks*. David & Charles, Newton Abbot, 1974.

Lee, John 'Babbacombe'. *'The Man They Could Not Hang': His Own Story*. Devon Books, Exeter, 1985.

St Leger-Gordon, Ruth E. *The Witchcraft and Folklore of Dartmoor*. 1965. Reprinted, Alan Sutton, Gloucester,1982.

Whitlock, Ralph. *The Folklore of Devon*. Batsford, London, 1977.

Wyatt, Monica. *Historic Inns of Devon*. Bossiney Books, Bodmin, 1990.

Index

Page numbers in italic refer to illustrations.

Amphion 42
Arthur, King 39
Baring-Gould, Rev. Sabine 27, 28, 34-5, 48
Baskervilles, The Hound of 16
Beast of Exmoor 26
Becket, Thomas à 13, 54
Betsy Grimbal's Tower 49, *49*
Black magic *see* Witchcraft
Blackingstone Rock *38*, 39
Blackmore, R. D. 18, 26, 27, 37
Bloody Corner 7
Blundell's School 11, 26
Body-snatching 48
Brutus Stone 50, *51*
Bull-baiting 51
Capel, Richard 16
Carew, Bampfylde Moore 11, *11*
Caves 15, 18, 36
Champernowne family 24, 40
Chantiloupe 12
Civil War 12, 19, 30, 35, 45, 51
Clerics 3, 7, 8, 13, 14, 26, 33, 33-4, 35, 40, 45, 48
Coffin Stone 24, *24*
Coo, Jan 24
Coppinger, Daniel/David 30
Crocker, Tom 18
Crossowen 50
Danes *see* Vikings
Dart, river 24, 47-8
Day's submarine 42
Devil 3, 8, 11, 14, 15, 25, 27, 36, 39, 41, 52, 53
Devil's Cauldron 36
Devil's footprints 28
Devil's Stone 46
Dewer 25, *25*, 29
Dragons 19
Drake, Sir Francis 17-18, 41
Dyer, Cutty 7
Elliott, Bob 'Resurrection' 15
Executions 7, 29, 41
Faggus, Tom 26, 45
Fairs and festivals 7, 30, 41
Fice's Well 44, *44*
Fitz family 48-9
Fitz's Well 40, *41*
Flood 37

Formidable 15-16
Forrest Hall 37
Gambling 22, 40, 51, 52
Geare, Benjie 22
Ghosts 3, *6*, *14*, 14-15, 18, 19, 25, 28, 30, 35, 45, 50, 53, 54.
  See also Geare, Benjie; Gould, Madam; Howard, Lady Mary; Knowles, Weaver; Long Strike; Spring-heeled Jack; Whisht Hounds
  animals (other than dogs) 13, 25, 30, 46, 47, 52
  aural 31, 45
  in carriages 16, 50
  child 28
  cleric 45
  dogs 12, 40, 52, 54
  dwarf 20
  horsemen 13, 23, 54
  lovers 10
  monks 16, 43
  omens 10, 23, 24, 47, 49
  soldier 8
  white ladies 10, 24
Giants 3, 7, 41, 49, 50
Gould, Madam 3, 34-5
Graves, memorials 11, *13*, 13-14, 15, 16, *16*, 18, 19-20, 20, 25, 31, *32*, *32*, 33, *33*, 38, 51
Grenville, Sir Richard 11
Grey, Lady Jane 32
Hairy hands 43
Herzogin Cecilie 45-6
Highwaymen 20, 26, 45
Hotel *see* Inns
Howard, Lady Mary 3, 40, 48-9
Human remains 12, 15, 16, 39
Inns, hotels 8, 18, *18*, 19, 20, *21*, 22, 27, *27*, 31, 34, 34-5, 37, 44, *44*, 47, *47*, 52, *52*
John & Lilley 14
Juba 14
King, Tom 45
Kingsley, Charles 36
Knowles, Weaver 17
Lee, John 7
Leprosy 50-1
Lich Way 36
Long Strike *6*, 35

Lorna Doone 18, 26, 37
Meldrum, Mother 26, 37-8
Memorials *see* Graves
Montagu 36
Murders 7, 10, 12, 13, 18, 20, 30, 40, 41-2, 49
Nine Maidens 9
Ogres *see* Giants
Oxenham family 47
Parsons *see* Clerics
Phantom cottages 17, 33
Pirates 8, 18, 35-6
Pixies 20, 29, 40, 44, 46
Plague 27, 49
Prehistoric remains 9, 19, 25, 26-7, *27*, 39, 47, 49, 54
Press-gang 8, 22
Prisons 36, 43, 43-4, 51
Puritans' Pit 40
Quarry 8
Radford, Jack 33
Raleigh, Walter 28
Rattenbury, John 8, *8*
Raybarrow Pool 47
Reynolds, Jan 52, 53
Road accidents 30, 42-3
Russell, Jack 48
'Salting down Feyther' 52
Smuggling 8, 13-14, 15, 18, 26, 30, 32, 35-6
Snaily House 8-9
Southcott, Joanna 3, *28*, 28-9
Spirit of the Ocean 48
Spring-heeled Jack 25
Statues 39, *39*, 41
Suicides 33, 36
Tin mining 22, 23, 25
Tombs *see* Graves
Tracy family 13, 54
Treasure 10, 19, 20, 30, 52
Trees 10, 31-2, *31*
Tunnels 8, 12, 27, 32, 47
Valley of the Rocks 37
Vampire 16
Vicars *see* Clerics
Vikings 7, 35
Wassailing 46
Westward Ho! 36
Whisht Hounds 16, 25, *25*, 43
Witchcraft 3, 7, 9, 27, 35, 38
Withrington, Jack 20
Wrecks, wrecking 12, 14, 32, 36, 37, 45-6, 48, 49-50, 53
Wrestling 21, 38